Great
Desserts
and Pastries

Great
Desserts
and Pastries

Robert Carrier

Hamlyn London · New York · Sydney · Toronto

Photographs in this series taken by Christian Délu, John Miller, Jack Nisberg, Iain Reid, Pipe-Rich
Design by Martin Atcherley for The Nassington Press Ltd.
Line drawings by Kate Simunek

Some material in this book has already been published in
The Robert Carrier Cookbook
Published in 1965 by
Thomas Nelson and Sons Ltd.
© Copyright Robert Carrier 1965

Published by
The Hamlyn Publishing Group Limited
London · New York · Sydney · Toronto
Astronaut House, Feltham, Middlesex, England

© Copyright Robert Carrier 1978

ISBN 0 600 32014 6

Printed in Italy

Contents

Notes on metrication

When making any of the recipes in this book, only follow one set of measures as they are not interchangeable.

In this book quantities are given in metric and Imperial measures. Exact conversion from Imperial to metric measures does not usually give very convenient working quantities and so the metric measures have been rounded off into units of 25 grams. The table below shows the recommended equivalents.

Ounces	Approx gram to nearest whole figure	Recommended conversion to nearest unit of 25
1	28	25
2	57	50
3	85	75
4	113	100
5	142	150
6	170	175
7	198	200
8	227	225
9	255	250
10	283	275
11	312	300
12	340	350
13	368	375
14	396	400
15	425	425
16 (1 lb)	454	450
17	482	475
18	510	500
19	539	550
20 (1¼ lb)	567	575

Note: When converting quantities over 20 oz first add the appropriate figures in the centre column, then adjust to the nearest unit of 25. As a general guide, 1 kg (1000 g) equals 2.2 lb or about 2 lb 3 oz. This method of conversion gives good results in nearly all cases, although in certain pastry and cake recipes a more accurate conversion is necessary to produce a balanced recipe.

Liquid measures

The millilitre has been used in this book and the following table gives a few examples.

Imperial	Approx ml to nearest whole figure	Recommended ml
¼ pint	142	150 ml
½ pint	283	300 ml
¾ pint	425	450 ml
1 pint	567	600 ml
1½ pints	851	900 ml
1¾ pints	992	1000 ml (1 litre)

Can sizes

At present, cans are marked with the exact (usually to the nearest whole number) metric equivalent of the Imperial weight of the contents, so we have followed this practice when giving can sizes.

Oven temperatures

The table below gives recommended equivalents.

	°C	°F	Gas Mark
Very cool	110	225	$\frac{1}{4}$
	120	250	$\frac{1}{2}$
Cool	140	275	1
	150	300	2
Moderate	160	325	3
	180	350	4
Moderately hot	190	375	5
	200	400	6
Hot	220	425	7
	230	450	8
Very hot	240	475	9

Notes for American and Australian users

In America the 8-oz measuring cup is used. In Australia metric measures are now used in conjunction with the standard 250-ml measuring cup. The Imperial pint, used in Britain and Australia, is 20 fl oz, while the American pint is 16 fl oz. It is important to remember that the Australian tablespoon differs from both the British and American tablespoons; the table below gives a comparison. The British standard tablespoon, which has been used throughout this book, holds 17.7 ml, the American 14.2 ml, and the Australian 20 ml. A teaspoon holds approximately 5 ml in all three countries.

British	American	Australian
1 teaspoon	1 teaspoon	1 teaspoon
1 tablespoon	1 tablespoon	1 tablespoon
2 tablespoons	3 tablespoons	2 tablespoons
$3\frac{1}{2}$ tablespoons	4 tablespoons	3 tablespoons
4 tablespoons	5 tablespoons	$3\frac{1}{2}$ tablespoons

An Imperial/American guide to solid and liquid measures

Solid measures

Imperial	American
1 lb butter or margarine	2 cups
1 lb flour	4 cups
1 lb granulated or castor sugar	2 cups
1 lb icing sugar	3 cups
8 oz rice	1 cup

Liquid measures

Imperial	American
$\frac{1}{4}$ pint liquid	$\frac{2}{3}$ cup liquid
$\frac{1}{2}$ pint	$1\frac{1}{4}$ cups
$\frac{3}{4}$ pint	2 cups
1 pint	$2\frac{1}{2}$ cups
$1\frac{1}{2}$ pints	$3\frac{3}{4}$ cups
2 pints	5 cups ($2\frac{1}{2}$ pints)

Introduction

My first arrival in England was not auspicious. On my twenty-first birthday I disembarked at Plymouth – an involuntary pilgrim – en route to the front. The invasion of Normandy had just taken place; the first casualties were beginning to be listed; flying bombs were roaring over London; and the English were tired. They seemed to have ceased to feel – the food was appalling and the war was welcomed as a God-given excuse for all the pent-up puritanism of the people to come to the fore. To serve unimaginative food was looked on almost as a virtue; to enjoy a meal, a sin.

How different it was when I reached France. Here the nightmare was over, and feasting – with that skilful logic the French apply to their own comfort – was considered a patriotic gesture. So it was in France I stayed. For six years I lived in St. Germain des Près, the most exciting quarter of what was then the most exciting city in the world: creative, young, experimental – ready for every new experience, whether philosophical or physical. But when I returned to England in 1953 for the Coronation, I might never have been here before, so different was it. Here was the Mrs. Miniver-land I had imagined in my childhood. London was *en fête*, buildings garlanded, crowds jubilant, pageantry to the fore.

One meal summed up the change for me – and led me to stretch my three weeks' visit to twelve years. I was asked to tea by Sir Stephen Tallents, well known for his evocations of the country life. The very name of his house was almost parody – St. John's Jerusalem. On my arrival, my host greeted me from the moat – knee-deep in water, rubber waders to the thighs, raking for the monastic relics that he discovered every now and then.

Then tea itself. No bread and jam and cakes, but mounds of fresh strawberries and cream – strawberries such as I had never tasted before – and when we had eaten our way through an absolute mountain of them, Sir Stephen rose from the table to return a few minutes later with another great bowl of the fruit, still hot from the sun, brushed clean, not washed. Perfection!

Featherlight Puddings

Most households in England had at least one recipe for a delicate pudding or a satin smooth cream which was truly their own speciality. These featherlight confections were not reserved for occasions – birthdays and anniversaries – but were served with pomp and pride at dinner parties throughout the year. Creamy baked custards made with fresh cream and eight egg yolks were deliciously flavoured with sugar, cinnamon and orange flower water; sharp gooseberries were whipped with cream and egg whites into frothy astringent fools and chocolate mousses vied with fresh fruit tanseys, burnt creams and extravagant rice moulds for top of the popularity poll.

To be memorable, autumn and winter sweets need not be elaborate or difficult. After a well-planned dinner the finest dessert imaginable is a plate of glistening ripe fruit: fresh golden peaches, fragrant grapes and apricots, crisp red and green apples, ripe, succulent pears. My grandmother used to spice peeled whole peaches and then bottle them in brandy-flavoured syrup. They were wonderful served chilled with lashings of whipped cream. Her fresh fruit pies were worth remembering, too, for she used to make, in place of a pastry cover, a sauce of double cream, brown sugar and a little flour; or dot the fruit slices with a crumble of flour, butter and sugar, that browned appetisingly during baking. Perhaps the most delicious memory of my childhood was the home-made vanilla and praline ice creams we used to eat in her snug country kitchen. My grandmother's version of this recipe – hand-turned in those days – was rich with her own farm eggs and double cream. Today I plump for the nursery sweets of those bygone days – and, judging from the menus at London's better restaurants, I am not alone.

Easy Fruit Desserts

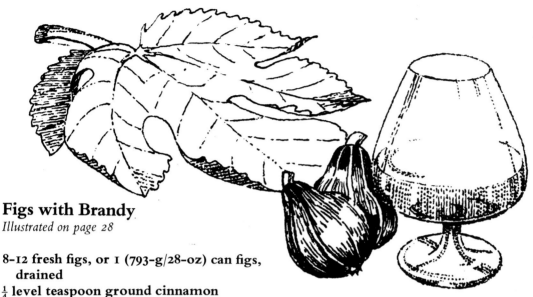

Figs with Brandy
Illustrated on page 28

8–12 fresh figs, or 1 (793-g/28-oz) can figs,
   drained
¼ level teaspoon ground cinnamon
1 level tablespoon grated orange rind
2–4 tablespoons brandy
4 tablespoons sherry
icing sugar (optional)
150 ml/¼ pint double cream, whipped
2 level tablespoons toasted almonds

1. Heat cinnamon, grated orange rind, brandy
and sherry, and sprinkle over figs. If figs are fresh,
add a little icing sugar, if required. Allow figs to
marinate in this flavouring for at least 1 hour
before serving.

2. Spoon whipped cream on to figs and garnish
with toasted almonds.

Pears in Chablis
Illustrated on page 66

12 small or 6 medium-sized pears
225 g/8 oz sugar
150 ml/¼ pint water
1–2 cinnamon sticks
150 ml/¼ pint Chablis, or other dry white
   wine
whipped cream

1. Peel pears but do not core them. Put them in a
saucepan with the sugar, water and cinnamon
sticks. Simmer, covered, for about 15 minutes.

Add Chablis and continue to cook over a low
heat, uncovered, for 15 minutes. Remove cinnamon sticks.

2. Put pears in a deep serving dish. Reduce liquid
to the consistency of a light syrup. Pour syrup
over the pears and chill. Serve very cold with
whipped cream.

Pears in Burgundy
Illustrated on page 25

12 small or 6 medium-sized pears
225 g/8 oz sugar
150 ml/¼ pint water
1–2 cinnamon sticks
150 ml/¼ pint red Burgundy
whipped cream

1. Peel pears but do not core them. Put them in a
saucepan with the sugar, water and cinnamon
sticks. Simmer, covered, for about 15 minutes.
Add Burgundy and continue to cook over a low
heat, uncovered, for 15 minutes. Remove cinnamon sticks.

2. Put pears in a deep serving dish. Reduce liquid
to the consistency of a light syrup. Pour syrup over
the pears and chill. Serve very cold with whipped
cream.

10

Transparent Apple Slices

4 Bramley seedlings
50 g/2 oz butter
4 tablespoons water
100-175 g/4-6 oz sugar
cinnamon

1. Peel, core and cut Bramley seedlings in thick slices.

2. Melt butter, add apple slices and water. Cover and allow to steam gently over a low heat until apple slices are almost tender – about 4 or 5 minutes.

3. Add sugar and sprinkle generously with cinnamon to taste. Cook, stirring gently, until apple slices are transparent and glazed with thick syrup.

4. Allow apple slices to cool, then serve.

Apple Hedgehog

6 medium-sized eating apples
225 g/8 oz granulated sugar
300 ml/½ pint water
grated rind of 1 lemon
1 kg/2 lb cooking apples
3 egg whites
castor sugar
icing sugar (optional)
24 almonds

1. Peel and core the eating apples, leaving them whole.

2. Combine granulated sugar with water and grated lemon rind in a saucepan. Bring to the boil and simmer apples in it gently until they are tender but not broken. Lift out and drain.

3. Peel, core and slice the cooking apples and cook them in the same syrup until reduced to a thick pulp.

4. Arrange the whole apples in a pyramid shape on a serving dish, spreading the apple pulp over them to make a smooth mound.

5. Whisk egg whites stiffly and fold in 2 tablespoons castor sugar.

6. Spread this meringue over the surface of the apples, covering them entirely, and sprinkle with a little more castor or icing sugar.

7. Blanch and split the almonds, and stick them here and there over the top. Brown meringue lightly in a moderately hot oven (190°C, 375°F, Gas Mark 5) for 5 to 10 minutes.

Blackberry Fool

675 g/1½ lb blackberries
150 ml/¼ pint water
100-225 g/4-8 oz sugar
150 ml/¼ pint Vanilla Custard Sauce (see page 91)
150 ml/¼ pint double cream, whipped

1. Wash blackberries and reserve 12 to 18 of the best. Put remainder in a saucepan with water and sugar. Cook until they are soft and then rub them through a fine sieve.

2. Mix vanilla custard and whipped cream (reserving a little cream for garnish) with the blackberry purée, and serve in a glass bowl or in individual glasses. Garnish with reserved blackberries and a swirl of whipped cream.

Rhubarb Fool

675 g/1½ lb young rhubarb
225 g/8 oz sugar
2 tablespoons lemon juice
4 level tablespoons butter
450 ml/¾ pint double cream, whipped
sugar or lemon juice

1. Wash and trim young rhubarb stalks and cut into 2.5-cm/1-inch segments.

Apple and Blackberry Fool *Serves 6 to 8*
Pineapple and Strawberries Romanov in the Shell
    Serves 4
Oranges Flambées *Serves 4*

2. Combine rhubarb, sugar, lemon juice and butter in a thick-bottomed saucepan and bring gently to the boil, stirring continuously. Lower heat and simmer, stirring all the time, for 5 to 8 minutes, until rhubarb is soft but still keeps its identity.

3. Whisk in an electric blender until smooth, or press through a fine sieve. Allow to cool, then chill in refrigerator until ready to use.

4. Just before serving, combine purée with whipped cream, and flavour to taste with sugar or lemon juice.

Apple and Blackberry Fool

1 kg/2 lb cooking apples
450 g/1 lb blackberries
100 g/4 oz granulated sugar
150 ml/¼ pint double cream, whipped
**150 ml/¼ pint Vanilla Custard Sauce (see
    page 91)**

1. Peel, core and slice apples. Wash blackberries and cook fruits with sugar to taste, in a little water until thoroughly softened.

2. Remove from the heat and sieve. Add more sugar if necessary and fold in whipped cream and vanilla custard. Turn into a glass bowl and decorate as desired.

Pineapple and Strawberries Romanov in the Shell

2 small pineapples
6 level tablespoons icing sugar
3 tablespoons Cointreau
3 tablespoons rum
300 ml/½ pint double cream
3 tablespoons Kirsch
8-12 strawberries
grated rind of 1 orange

1. Slice the pineapples in half lengthwise. With a sharp knife remove pineapple flesh, leaving a shell about 5 mm/¼ inch thick. Refrigerate shells

until ready to use. Slice pineapple, removing the hard central core, and cut into segments.

2. Toss segments with 4 level tablespoons icing sugar. Arrange segments in a bowl suitable for serving at the table, and pour over them a mixture of Cointreau and rum. Chill in the refrigerator until ready to use.

3. One hour before serving, whip cream, add remaining icing sugar and flavour with Kirsch. Spoon whipped cream into marinated pineapple pieces, tossing until every piece is coated with creamy liqueur mixture.

4. Pile prepared pineapple pieces into reserved shells, garnish with strawberries, top with finely grated orange rind and serve immediately.

Oranges Flambées

4 large oranges
350 g/12 oz sugar
4 tablespoons Grand Marnier

1. Remove bright outer peel carefully from oranges with a fruit parer. Cut into matchstick-sized pieces and reserve. Remove remaining pith from oranges and separate each orange into 8 segments.

2. Melt sugar in a small thick-bottomed saucepan, and stir over a low heat until it is a good caramel colour.

3. Spear each orange segment with a fork and dip into caramel mixture. Place caramel-glazed orange segments thin sides up in a metal serving dish.

4. Stir *julienne* of orange matchsticks into caramel sauce and cook over a very low heat, stirring constantly.

5. Drain and garnish each glazed orange section with caramelised matchsticks of orange.

6. When ready to serve, heat metal serving dish and flame with Grand Marnier. Serve immediately.

Summer Fruit Cup *Serves 6 to 8*
Summer Pudding under a Blanket *Serves 6 to 8*
Quick Fruit Compote in Wine *Serves 4 to 6*

12

Summer Fruit Cup

225-350 g/8-12 oz strawberries
225-350 g/8-12 oz raspberries
2 bananas, sliced
225 g/8 oz redcurrants or whitecurrants
100 g/4 oz loaf sugar
150 ml/¼ pint water
6 tablespoons claret or Burgundy
1 tablespoon brandy
2 level tablespoons chopped pistachio nuts
   or shredded coconut
whipped cream and biscuits (optional)

1. Prepare fruits and mix lightly in a glass bowl.

2. Boil the sugar and water together until they form a syrup; skim if necessary.

3. Allow the syrup to cool, then add wine and brandy, and pour over fruit. Stand in a cool place for several hours.

4. Just before serving, sprinkle nuts or coconut over the top. Whipped cream and biscuits may be served separately.

Summer Pudding under a Blanket

225 g/8 oz redcurrants or blackcurrants
350 g/12 oz cherries
225 g/8 oz raspberries
150 ml/¼ pint water
100-175 g/4-6 oz sugar
7-8 thin slices white bread
double cream, whipped
ripe cherries or raspberries to decorate

1. Strip all stalks from currants, stone cherries, combine with raspberries and wash if necessary.

2. Place fruits with water and sugar in a saucepan, and simmer gently until sugar melts.

3. Trim crusts from bread, cut each slice in half lengthwise and line sides of a 1-litre/1½-pint pudding basin or soufflé dish with bread. Cover

bottom of dish with triangles of bread, and trim off bread slices at top edge of dish.

4. Fill dish with fruit mixture. Cut additional bread triangles to cover pudding. Place a flat plate on pudding, weight it and chill in refrigerator overnight.

5. When ready to serve, turn out pudding on to a moistened serving dish and pipe top and sides of pudding with whipped cream. Decorate with ripe cherries or raspberries.

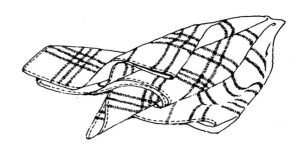

Quick Fruit Compote in Wine

4 canned pineapple rings
4 canned whole peaches
4 canned whole mirabelles or golden plums
1 (213-g/7½-oz) can apricots
1 (225-g/8-oz) can green figs
1 (312-g/11-oz) can lychees (optional)
fresh strawberries (optional)
finely grated orange peel

SAUCE
4 level tablespoons brown sugar
2 level tablespoons butter
300 ml/½ pint rosé wine
2 cloves
½ cinnamon stick

1. Drain canned fruits from syrup with a slotted spoon, reserving syrup for another use. Cut pineapple rings into halves or quarters and combine in a serving bowl with whole peaches, mirabelles, apricots and green figs. Garnish with a few canned lychees and fresh strawberries, if desired. Chill.

2. Combine sugar, butter and rosé wine in a small saucepan and add cloves and cinnamon. Bring to the boil and cook until reduced and slightly thickened. Pour over fruits, sprinkle with finely grated orange peel and return to refrigerator until required.

Macedoine of Fruit

1 stale Madeira or sponge cake
175 g/6 oz butter
675 g/1½ lb pears
1 (339-g/12-oz) can pineapple pieces
12 canned or glacé cherries
25 g/1 oz granulated sugar
little rum or Kirsch

1. Cut the sponge cake into 2 layers. Cut each layer into thin strips.

2. Melt 100 g/4 oz of the butter in a shallow pan and lightly fry the cake strips, remove and arrange some decoratively round a shallow dish. Dice remainder and pile in centre of dish.

3. Peel, slice and core the pears and lightly fry in the remainder of the butter together with the drained pineapple pieces. Mix with the cherries and spoon fruits into the centre of the dish.

4. Add granulated sugar to the pineapple juice with a little rum or Kirsch and cook until thick. Pour over the fruit and serve.

Port Wine or Claret Jellies

300 ml/½ pint water
100 g/4 oz sugar
2 level tablespoons redcurrant jelly
2.5-cm/1-inch stick cinnamon
3 cloves
rind and juice of 1 lemon
25 g/1 oz gelatine
300 ml/½ pint port or claret
2–3 drops of red food colouring (optional)
whipped cream (optional)

1. Combine water, sugar, redcurrant jelly, cinnamon stick and cloves in a saucepan. Add very thinly peeled lemon rind, strained lemon juice,

and gelatine which you have dissolved in a little water. Stir over heat until gelatine is dissolved. Simmer very gently for a few minutes, then add port or claret. Do not allow to boil again.

2. Strain through a piece of muslin and, if necessary, add a few drops of red food colouring to improve colour. Cool.

3. When almost cold, pour into small individual moulds that have been rinsed out with cold water. Chill until firm. Turn out when ready to serve, and decorate with whipped cream if desired.

Orange Jelly Quarters

5 thin-skinned oranges
150 ml/¼ pint port
15 g/½ oz powdered gelatine
150 ml/¼ pint water
1 lemon
100 g/4 oz sugar
sponge fingers and cream (optional)

1. Wash oranges well, pare 1 orange very thinly and infuse peel in port for 1 hour.

2. Soak gelatine in half the water, stir over a low heat until dissolved.

3. Slice remaining oranges in half, and scoop out pulp and juices, reserving orange shells. Discard pips. Combine juice and pulp of all oranges and the lemon with sugar and remaining water.

4. Strain dissolved gelatine and port into orange mixture.

5. Fill emptied orange shells with mixture, cool and chill. When set, cut into halves again. Serve alone, or with sponge fingers and cream.

13

14

Poached Pear Zabaglione

**6 small pears poached in white wine (see
    Pears in Chablis, page 9)
syrup from pears
3 egg yolks
40 g/1½ oz castor sugar
a little grated lemon rind peel
6-8 tablespoons Marsala, Madeira or sherry**

1. Place cold poached pears in individual sorbet glasses with a little of the syrup.

2. To make zabaglione sauce: beat egg yolks and castor sugar together in a mixing bowl. Add a little grated lemon rind and pour mixture into the top of a double saucepan. Place over simmering water and beat mixture until frothy.

3. Add Marsala, Madeira or sherry, a little at a time, and beat until the sauce is thick and smooth.

4. Pour sauce over cold poached pears and serve.

Brandied Pears

**1 kg/2 lb sugar
1 teaspoon vanilla essence
1 long strip lemon peel
2 cloves
1.15 litres/2 pints water
2.75 kg/6 lb ripe pears
600 ml/1 pint brandy**

1. Combine sugar, vanilla essence, lemon peel, cloves and water in large saucepan, and bring to the boil, stirring constantly. Lower heat and simmer, uncovered for 15 minutes.

2. Peel, halve and core pears. Add them to syrup and simmer gently, uncovered, for 30 to 40 minutes, until pears are translucent and soft. Remove from syrup with a slotted spoon.

3. Sterilise 4 600-ml/1-pint jars and leave in hot water until ready to fill.

4. Place 4 tablespoons brandy in each hot jar. Half-fill jars with drained pears, add 2 tablespoons

brandy to each jar. Fill jars with remaining pears, add 2 final tablespoons brandy, and fill with strained syrup to within 1 cm/½ inch of top. Seal jars and store.

Orange Slices Ambrosia

**4-6 oranges
4 tablespoons Curaçao
4 tablespoons lemon juice
6 level tablespoons freshly grated coconut**

1. Peel oranges, removing all white pith, and separate into segments. Marinate orange segments overnight in Curaçao and lemon juice.

2. Arrange orange segments in a shallow glass serving dish. Pour marinade juices over them and sprinkle with freshly grated coconut.

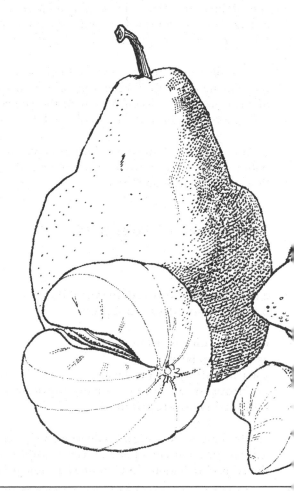

Sherried Prunes

1–1.5 kg/2–3 lb dried prunes
1 kg/2 lb sugar
1 teaspoon vanilla essence
4 lemon slices
2 cloves
1.15 litres/2 pints water
1 bottle sherry
whipped cream
Vanilla Custard Sauce (see page 91)

1. Soak prunes overnight in cold water. Drain.

2. Combine sugar, vanilla essence, lemon slices, cloves and water in a large saucepan, and bring to the boil, stirring constantly. Lower heat and simmer, uncovered, for 15 minutes.

3. Add prunes to sugar syrup and simmer gently, uncovered, adding more water if necessary, for 30 to 40 minutes, or until prunes are almost cooked

through. Remove prunes from syrup with a slotted spoon.

4. Sterilise 4 600-ml/1-pint jars, leave in hot water until ready to fill. Fill jars almost to the top with drained prunes. Half-fill each jar with sherry and add strained syrup to cover. Seal jars and store.

To serve sherried prunes as a dessert: chill prunes in their liqueur. Serve with accompanying sauce boats of whipped cream and vanilla custard.

Baked Pear Compote

1 kg/2 lb firm pears
butter
rind and juice of 1 lemon
175 g/6 oz brown sugar
double cream

1. Peel, slice and core pears, and place in a buttered ovenproof baking dish. Sprinkle the slices with lemon juice, grated lemon rind, brown sugar and dot with butter.

2. Bake uncovered in a moderately hot oven (190°C, 375°F, Gas Mark 5) for 30 minutes, or until tender. Serve with double cream.

Rum Baked Pears in Cream

6 pears
butter
3 tablespoons rum
3 tablespoons water
175 g/6 oz sugar
½ level teaspoon cinnamon
¼ level teaspoon freshly ground nutmeg
150 ml/¼ pint double cream

1. Wash, peel, core and thinly slice the pears and arrange them in a well-buttered ovenproof baking dish. Dot with butter.

2. Combine remaining ingredients, pour over apples and bake in a moderately hot oven (190°C, 375°F, Gas Mark 5) for 30 minutes, or until tender. Serve hot.

Water Ices, Sorbets and Ice Creams

16

Syrup for Water Ices

225 g/8 oz sugar
600 ml/1 pint water
juice of ½ lemon

Combine sugar and water in a saucepan, bring to the boil and boil for 10 minutes, removing any scum that rises. Cool to lukewarm, add lemon juice and strain through a muslin-lined sieve.

Strawberry Water Ice

300 ml/½ pint strawberry purée (see step 2)
300 ml/½ pint syrup for water ices (see above)
juice of 1 lemon, strained
red food colouring
2 egg whites

1. Turn refrigerator to its lowest temperature (i.e. highest setting).

2. Rub enough ripe strawberries through a hair sieve to make 300 ml/½ pint of puréed fruit.

3. Combine fruit purée, syrup, strained lemon juice, and enough red food colouring to make a pink ice.

4. When quite cold, pour mixture into freezing tray or loaf tin and freeze, stirring the mixture vigorously with a fork every 30 minutes, until half-frozen.

5. Whisk egg whites until stiff and stir into the half-frozen mixture.

6. Continue freezing until the ice is sufficiently stiff for serving.

Pineapple Water Ice

Illustrated on page 46

1 (376-g/13¼-oz) can pineapple slices
300 ml/½ pint syrup for water ices (see above)
juice of 1 lemon, strained
vanilla essence or Kirsch
yellow food colouring

1. Turn refrigerator to its lowest temperature (i.e. highest setting).

2. Chop the pineapple and pound it in a mortar with a little juice from the can. Rub it through a fine sieve. To 300 ml/½ pint of this purée add 300 ml/½ pint syrup, the strained lemon juice and vanilla essence or a little Kirsch. Tint with a little yellow food colouring.

3. When cold, pour mixture into a freezing tray

or loaf tin and freeze, stirring the mixture vigorously with a fork every 30 minutes, until half-frozen, then leaving it for a further 2 or 3 hours until frozen solid. Transfer water ice to main cabinet of refrigerator about 1 hour before serving. Serve water ice piled up in individual iced serving dishes.

Grape Water Ice

450 g/1 lb muscat grapes
300 ml/½ pint syrup for water ices (see page 16)
juice of 2 lemons
1 tablespoon orange flower water
3 tablespoons Marsala

1. Turn refrigerator to its lowest temperature (i.e. highest setting).

2. Wash grapes, crush them and rub them through a hair sieve.

3. Strain syrup and lemon juice over the grape purée, add orange flower water and Marsala and allow to cool.

4. Pour mixture into freezing tray and freeze, stirring the mixture vigorously with a fork every 30 minutes, until half-frozen, then leaving it for a further 2 or 3 hours until frozen hard. Transfer water ice to main cabinet of refrigerator about 1 hour before serving.

5. Serve water ice piled up in small cups.

Blackcurrant Sorbet

600 ml/1 pint blackcurrants, topped and tailed
juice of 2 lemons, strained
75-100 g/3-4 oz granulated sugar

1. Turn refrigerator to its lowest temperature (i.e. highest setting).

2. Place half the blackcurrants in an electric blender and blend for a few seconds until puréed.

Repeat the process with the remaining currants, and add them to the first purée.

3. Add the strained lemon juice to the sugar and stir well. Add to the fruit purée.

4. Pour mixture into freezing tray and freeze until almost stiff, about 1 hour.

5. Put half the blackcurrant ice in the blender and blend until softened to sorbet consistency. Repeat with second half. Spoon into chilled glasses and serve at once.

Tangerine Sorbet with Lychees

Illustrated on page 48

175 g/6 oz castor sugar
300 ml/½ pint water
finely grated rind and juice of 8 tangerines
finely grated rind and juice of 1 large lemon
1 egg white, stiffly beaten
lychees
mandarin orange segments
toasted almond spikes

1. Turn refrigerator to its lowest temperature (i.e. highest setting).

2. To make sorbet: dissolve the sugar in the water and then boil rapidly for 5 minutes. Add the rind and juice of the tangerines and lemon and leave to cool. When cold, strain into a deep freezing tray (I often use a loaf tin) and place in the ice-making compartment of the refrigerator. Freeze for 1 hour.

3. Remove from the tray, beat well and then return to the freezer for 1 hour, then fold in the stiffly beaten egg white and beat well. Freeze until firm and set.

4. To serve: spoon sorbet into individual dishes and top with lychees and orange segments. Spike with almonds.

17

Vanilla Ice Cream

4 egg yolks
100 g/4 oz sugar
pinch of salt
450 ml/¾ pint single cream
1-2 teaspoons vanilla essence

1. Turn refrigerator to its lowest temperature (i.e. highest setting) about 1 hour before you make ice cream.

2. Beat egg yolks, sugar and salt until light and lemon-coloured.

3. Scald single cream, and add to egg and sugar mixture, whisking until mixture is well blended.

4. Pour mixture into top of a double saucepan and cook over water, stirring continuously, until custard coats spoon.

5. Strain mixture through a fine sieve and stir in vanilla essence.

6. Pour mixture into containers of your choice and put in freezing compartment. Stir mixture every 30 minutes until it is semi-frozen, then leave for 2 or 3 hours, until it is frozen.

Apricot Ice Cream

300 ml/½ pint apricot purée (see step 2)
300 ml/½ pint double cream, lightly whipped
lemon juice
2-3 tablespoons apricot liqueur
2-3 drops of red food colouring
castor sugar

1. Turn refrigerator to its lowest temperature (i.e. highest setting) about 1 hour before you make ice cream.

2. Make the apricot purée by rubbing canned apricots through a hair sieve, using some of the syrup. The purée must not be too thick.

3. Mix the lightly whipped cream into the purée, then add lemon juice, apricot liqueur and enough red food colouring to give the mixture a good apricot colour. Sweeten to taste.

4. Pour mixture into containers of your choice and put in freezing compartment. Stir mixture every 30 minutes until it is semi-frozen, then leave for 2 or 3 hours, until it is frozen.

Note: Fresh apricots may be used, but they must be stewed until soft in a syrup of sugar and water, before serving.

Liqueur Ice Cream

600 ml/1 pint double cream
100 g/4 oz castor sugar
Maraschino or other liqueur

1. Turn refrigerator to its lowest temperature (i.e. highest setting) about 1 hour before you make ice cream.

2. Whip cream and add sugar. Flavour to taste with Maraschino or liqueur of your choice. Mix well.

3. Pour mixture into containers of your choice and put in freezing compartment. Stir mixture every 30 minutes until it is semi-frozen, then leave for 2 or 3 hours, until it is frozen.

Banana Ice Cream

5 bananas, peeled and sliced
4 egg yolks
100 g/4 oz sugar
pinch of salt
450 ml/¾ pint single cream
1-2 teaspoons vanilla essence
grated rind and juice of 1 orange
150 ml/¼ pint double cream, whipped
castor sugar
1-2 tablespoons Maraschino or other liqueur
yellow food colouring (optional)

1. Turn refrigerator to its lowest temperature (i.e. highest setting) about 1 hour before you make ice cream.

2. Beat egg yolks, sugar and salt until light and lemon-coloured.

3. Scald single cream, and add to egg and sugar mixture, whisking until mixture is well blended.

4. Pour mixture into top of a double saucepan and cook over water, stirring continuously, until custard coats spoon.

5. Strain mixture through a fine sieve and stir in vanilla essence. Flavour custard with grated orange rind.

6. Rub ripe bananas through a sieve to make 150 ml/$\frac{1}{4}$ pint banana purée. Add strained orange juice, chilled custard and whipped double cream to banana purée, and flavour to taste with castor sugar and 1 or 2 tablespoons Maraschino or other liqueur. Colour slightly if desired with yellow food colouring.

7. Pour mixture into containers of your choice and put in freezing compartment. Stir mixture every 30 minutes until it is semi-frozen, then leave for 2 or 3 hours, until it is frozen.

20

Tangerine Ice Cream

6 tangerines
100 g/4 oz castor sugar
600 ml/1 pint double cream

1. Turn refrigerator to its lowest temperature (i.e. highest setting) about 1 hour before you make ice cream.

2. Grate the rind of 3 tangerines very lightly and rub rind into the sugar. Put this flavoured sugar in the top of a double saucepan with half the cream, and scald until sugar is quite dissolved. Remove from the heat and cool.

3. Strain the juice of the 6 tangerines into the mixture.

4. Whip remaining cream and fold into mixture.

5. Pour mixture into containers of your choice and put in freezing compartment. Stir every 30 minutes until it is semi-frozen, then leave for 2 or 3 hours, until it is frozen.

Biscuit Tortoni

Illustrated on page 48

300 ml/½ pint double cream
2 egg whites
castor sugar
salt
100 g/4 oz chopped toasted almonds
sherry, Marsala or cognac

1. Turn refrigerator to its lowest temperature (i.e. highest setting) about 1 hour before you make ice cream.

2. Whip cream.

3. Whisk egg whites, add sugar and salt to taste, and continue whisking until mixture is stiff and glossy.

4. Fold chopped almonds (reserving 2 tablespoons for garnish) into egg mixture with whipped cream.

5. Stir in sherry, Marsala or cognac, to taste, and spoon mixture into 6 to 8 individual soufflé dishes or custard cups. Sprinkle with reserved almonds and put in freezing compartment; leave for 2 or 3 hours, until it is frozen.

Ice Cream with Summer Fruits

225 g/8 oz fresh raspberries
225 g/8 oz redcurrants
225 g/8 oz blackberries
4-6 scoops Vanilla Ice Cream (see page 18)
4-6 tablespoons Poire liqueur or Kirsch

1. Clean and prepare fruits. Chill in refrigerator.

2. Place 1 scoop of ice cream in each individual *coupe* or champagne glass. Sprinkle with 1 tablespoon *Poire* liqueur or Kirsch.

3. Cover ice cream with chilled fruits and serve immediately.

Praline Ice Cream

100 g/4 oz almonds
225 g/8 oz sugar
few drops of lemon juice
oil
4 egg yolks
pinch of salt
450 ml/¾ pint single cream
1-2 teaspoons vanilla essence
300 ml/½ pint double cream
liqueur or cognac

1. Turn refrigerator to its lowest temperature (i.e. highest setting) about 1 hour before you make ice cream.

2. Blanch almonds, chop them roughly and dry well.

3. Combine half the sugar in a small saucepan with

lemon juice and melt it carefully over a medium heat until it takes on a good caramel colour. Add chopped almonds and stir constantly until they are golden brown.

4. Pour the mixture on to a flat tin that has been greased with olive oil, and let it cool.

5. Beat egg yolks, remaining sugar and salt until light and lemon-coloured.

6. Scald single cream, and add to egg and sugar mixture, whisking until mixture is well blended.

7. Pour mixture into top of a double saucepan and cook over water, stirring continuously, until custard coats spoon.

8. Strain mixture through a fine sieve and stir in vanilla essence.

9. When praline mixture is cold and hard, reduce it to a powder by pounding it in a mortar. Add this powder to the warm custard.

10. Pour mixture into containers of your choice and put in freezing compartment. Stir mixture every 30 minutes until it is semi-frozen.

11. Whip double cream, fold into custard with a little liqueur or cognac, and freeze for 2 or 3 hours, until it is frozen.

Christmas Snowball Bombe

21

4 level tablespoons diced candied cherries
4 level tablespoons diced candied pineapple
4 level tablespoons diced candied citron
3 level tablespoons dried sultanas
2 level tablespoons dried currants
Kirsch
900 ml/1½ pints Vanilla Ice Cream (see page 18)
600 ml/1 pint double cream
½ teaspoon vanilla essence
sugar
crystallised violets
small holly leaves

1. Soak all fruits in 6 tablespoons Kirsch for 2 hours, stirring from time to time.

2. Combine fruits and liqueur with softened vanilla ice cream and mix well. Pack mixture into a round *bombe* mould (or fill 2 small pudding basins and press together to form sphere) and freeze until solid.

3. Just before serving, unmould 'snowball' on to a chilled serving dish. Whip cream and flavour with vanilla essence, sugar and Kirsch, to taste. Place in a piping bag fitted with a 'rosette' nozzle. Mask ice cream completely with rosettes of whipped cream and decorate with crystallised violets and small holly leaves.

Creams, Custards and Baked Puddings

22

Caramel Cream

Illustrated on page 28

4 egg yolks
castor sugar
600 ml/1 pint double cream

1. Beat egg yolks with 4 tablespoons castor sugar until light and frothy.

2. Bring cream to the boil and boil for 1 minute, then pour over the egg yolks. Pour this custard into the dish in which it is to be served. Allow it to cool, then chill in refrigerator.

3. Just before serving, sprinkle a layer of castor sugar 3 mm/$\frac{1}{8}$ inch thick on top, and brown it quickly under a preheated grill. The grill must be very hot to caramelise the surface.

Baked Custard Pudding à l'Orange

4 egg yolks
2 egg whites
4 tablespoons castor sugar
pinch of salt
$\frac{1}{2}$ teaspoon vanilla essence
600 ml/1 pint milk
grated rind and juice of $\frac{1}{2}$ orange
1-2 tablespoons Grand Marnier
butter

1. Beat the egg yolks and whites in a bowl with castor sugar, salt and vanilla essence.

2. Heat the milk and freshly grated orange rind, without allowing it to boil, and pour slowly over the beaten eggs, stirring constantly. Beat in orange juice and Grand Marnier and strain the mixture into a well-buttered 1-litre/1$\frac{1}{2}$-pint soufflé dish, or into individual buttered ramekins.

3. Place the dish, or ramekins, in a baking tin two-thirds full of hot water, and cook in a moderately hot oven (190°C, 375°F, Gas Mark 5) for about 1 hour, or until the custard sets and the top is golden brown. Sprinkle custard with a little castor sugar.

Baked Bread and Butter Pudding

Illustrated on page 68

2-4 slices bread
softened butter
2 eggs
600 ml/1 pint milk
castor sugar
vanilla essence
4 level tablespoons currants or sultanas

1. Remove crusts from bread, butter slices, and cut into thin strips. Lay bread strips in a well-buttered oblong ovenproof dish. The dish should be about half full.

2. Whisk eggs in a mixing bowl, add the milk, and sugar and vanilla essence to taste. Mix well together and strain over bread strips. Allow pudding to stand until bread is well soaked.

3. Sprinkle with currants or sultanas. Bake in a moderately hot oven (190°C, 375°F, Gas Mark 5) for 20 to 30 minutes until golden brown and firm to the touch. Sprinkle with sugar and serve hot.

Brown Betty

675 g/1$\frac{1}{2}$ lb apples, peeled, cored and sliced
butter
175 g/6 oz browned breadcrumbs
3 level tablespoons golden syrup
150 ml/$\frac{1}{4}$ pint water
$\frac{1}{2}$ level teaspoon ground cinnamon
sugar
cream

1. Place a layer of sliced apples in a buttered pie dish. Sprinkle some of the breadcrumbs over them, and dot with butter. Put in some more apples and repeat these alternate layers until all the apples and breadcrumbs are used up, finishing with a top layer of breadcrumbs.

2. Mix syrup with water and cinnamon, and pour this over the top of the apples. Sprinkle with sugar and dot with butter.

3. Place the pie dish in a baking tin two-thirds full of hot water, and bake in a moderately hot oven (190°C, 375°F, Gas Mark 5) for 1 hour, or until the apples are soft. Serve with cream.

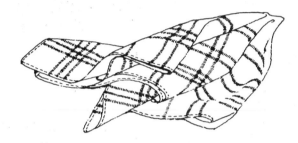

Apple Amber Pudding

675 g/1½ lb apples, peeled, cored and sliced
2-4 level tablespoons granulated sugar
4 level tablespoons butter
grated rind of 1 lemon
2 egg yolks, beaten
1 quantity shortcrust pastry (see page 58)
2 egg whites
1 level tablespoon castor sugar
vanilla essence
glacé cherries
angelica

1. Combine apples, sugar, butter and grated lemon rind in a saucepan, and simmer gently, stirring from time to time, until mixture is reduced to pulp. Beat mixture with a wooden spoon until perfectly smooth, or rub it through a sieve, then add beaten egg yolks.

2. Line a large deep pie dish with shortcrust pastry and pour apple mixture into it. Bake in a moderately hot oven (190°C, 375°F, Gas Mark 5) for 30 to 40 minutes, until the pastry is cooked and the apple mixture set.

3. Whisk egg whites until stiff and flavour with 1 tablespoon castor sugar and a few drops of vanilla.

4. Pile meringue on top of the pudding and decorate with a few pieces of glacé cherry and angelica. Return to a cool oven (150°C, 300°F, Gas Mark 2) for 10 to 15 minutes until lightly browned.

Queen of Puddings

50 g/2 oz fresh breadcrumbs
3 tablespoons butter
3-4 level tablespoons sugar
grated lemon rind
vanilla essence
600 ml/1 pint milk
3 egg yolks
3-4 level tablespoons apricot or strawberry jam
lemon juice

MERINGUE
4 egg whites
castor sugar

1. Combine breadcrumbs with butter and sugar. Flavour to taste with grated lemon rind and vanilla essence.

2. Bring the milk almost to the boil in a small saucepan. Pour it over the crumb mixture and let it soak for 10 minutes.

3. Stir in egg yolks, pour the mixture into a well-buttered large deep pie dish and bake in a moderately hot oven (190°C, 375°F, Gas Mark 5) for 20 to 25 minutes, until set. Remove from oven and allow to cool.

4. When cool, spread with apricot or strawberry jam flavoured to taste with lemon juice.

5. Beat egg whites until stiff but not dry, fold in castor sugar to taste.

6. Pile meringue on pudding in high peaks and bake in a moderate oven (180°C, 350°F, Gas Mark 4) until meringue is lightly browned.

24

Baked Sultana Pudding

225 g/8 oz plain flour
salt
1 level teaspoon baking powder
6 tablespoons butter or lard
75 g/3 oz sultanas
3 level tablespoons sugar
little candied peel, finely shredded
1 teaspoon vanilla essence
2 eggs, well beaten
175 ml/6 fl oz milk
cream

1. Sift the flour, salt and baking powder into a bowl, and rub in butter or lard until free from lumps.

2. Pick and clean the sultanas, and add them with the sugar, candied peel and vanilla essence. Make a well in the centre, add the beaten eggs, and then gradually mix in the milk. Mix together thoroughly.

3. Put the mixture in a well-buttered deep oven-proof dish about 38 by 23 cm/15 by 9 inches, and bake in a moderately hot oven (190°C, 375°F, Gas Mark 5) for 30 minutes, or until well risen and firm to the touch.

3. To serve: cut into squares, sprinkle with additional sugar and serve hot with cream.

Baked Apricot Roll

225 g/8 oz plain flour
1 level teaspoon baking powder
1 level teaspoon salt
1-2 level tablespoons castor sugar
100 g/4 oz shredded suet
6-8 tablespoons water
350 g/12 oz apricot jam
butter
Vanilla Custard Sauce (see page 91) or
   whipped cream

1. Combine flour, baking powder, salt, sugar and suet in a large mixing bowl. Work suet into dry ingredients with fingertips. Mix in enough water

(6 to 8 tablespoons) with a fork to make dough leave sides of the bowl.

2. Roll dough into an oblong about 30 by 45 cm/12 by 18 inches. Spread with apricot jam and roll lengthwise into a large sausage shape. Seal edge with water and fold ends like an envelope.

3. Place roll in a large buttered baking tin and bake in a hot oven (220°C, 425°F, Gas Mark 7) for 20 to 30 minutes, until golden.

4. Serve warm with Vanilla Custard Sauce or whipped cream.

Cottage Pudding

275 g/10 oz plain flour
2 level teaspoons baking powder
½ level teaspoon salt
6 level tablespoons softened butter
½ teaspoon vanilla essence
150 g/5 oz sugar
2 eggs
250 ml/8 fl oz milk
Lemon or Strawberry Hard Sauce (see
   page 91)

1. Sift flour, baking powder and salt into a mixing bowl.

2. Work softened butter and vanilla essence together until soft, add sugar gradually and continue beating until mixture is creamy.

3. Separate eggs and beat yolks thoroughly into creamed mixture. Stir in a third of the flour mixture and add a third of the milk. Repeat these ingredients alternately, ending with flour, until all ingredients are used.

4. Beat egg whites until stiff and fold gently into batter.

5. Pour batter into a greased 1.25-litre/2-pint pudding basin and bake in a moderate oven (180°C, 350°F, Gas Mark 4) for 30 to 40 minutes. Cool slightly and serve topped with Lemon or Strawberry Hard Sauce.

Pears in Burgundy (see page 9)

Summer Fruit Harvest

Fresh Fruit Salad
Figs with Brandy (see page 9)
Caramel Cream (see page 22)

Gâteau de Pommes à la Crème

1½ quantity shortcrust pastry (see page 58)
butter
finely chopped almonds
melted apricot jam

APPLE FILLING
2 sheets leaf gelatine or 7 g/¼ oz powdered
  gelatine
300 ml/½ pint lemon or wine jelly
150 ml/¼ pint double cream, whipped
300 ml/½ pint thick apple purée
1 tablespoon liqueur

TO DECORATE
300 ml/½ pint double cream, whipped,
  sweetened and flavoured
diced preserved fruits

1. Make shortcrust pastry as directed.

2. Butter a 1-litre/1½-pint soufflé mould and line
it with shortcrust pastry, rolled out very thinly.
Prick dough with a fork; chill in the refrigerator
for 2 hours. Then line the mould with foil, fill
with rice or dried haricot beans and bake 'blind'
in a moderately hot oven (200°C, 400°F, Gas
Mark 4) for about 15 minutes, or until pastry is
thoroughly cooked. Reduce heat to moderate
(180°C, 350°F, Gas Mark 4); then remove foil
and rice or beans, and return the pastry case to
the oven for 5 to 10 minutes to dry and brown
inside. **Note:** if pastry begins to brown at edges,
cover edges with a little foil. When cooked, turn
it out carefully and cool on a wire tray.

3. Brown finely chopped almonds in the oven.

4. Brush outside of the pastry case with melted
apricot jam, and coat it with finely chopped
almonds.

5. To make apple filling: soak gelatine (see
Rice à la Royale, page 35, step 3) and then dissolve
in lemon or wine jelly to make it extra stiff.
Strain mixture into a mixing bowl and whisk
until white and frothy. Stir whipped cream into
jelly and fold into thick apple purée. Add liqueur
or other flavouring, to taste, and when mixture

is on the point of setting, pour it into the pastry
case. Set aside to cool for at least 30 minutes.

6. To finish: have whipped cream, sweetened
and flavoured, ready in a piping bag fitted with a
rose pipe. Pipe whipped cream 'rosettes' into top
of *gâteau* and decorate with diced preserved fruits.

Coeur à la Crème

175 g/6 oz cream cheese
1 egg yolk
2 level tablespoons sugar
grated rind of 1 orange
1 teaspoon vanilla essence
salt
200 ml/7 fl oz double cream
fresh berries of your choice: strawberries,
  blueberries, raspberries, etc.

1. Beat the cream cheese until very light and fluffy.
Then beat in egg yolk, sugar, grated orange rind,
vanilla essence and a generous pinch of salt.

2. Whip the cream with a large whisk until the
cream holds its shape. Fold the cream into the
cream cheese mixture with a spatula.

3. Cut squares of cheesecloth (double thickness)
large enough to come about 3.5 cm/1½ inches outside each heart-shaped mould when used as a
lining. Moisten with cold water, wring out, then
carefully line each heart-shaped dish.

4. Fill the cheesecloth-lined dishes with the cheese
mixture, piling mixture into a slight dome in each
dish. Fold over ends of cheesecloth to cover cheese.
Place the moulds on a wire tray placed over a
baking tin to drain in the refrigerator overnight.

5. To serve: unmould 1 delicate cheese 'heart' on
to each dessert plate. Fill each heart-shaped mould
(which you have first washed and dried) with
chilled fresh berries, and place on each plate beside
the moulded *coeur à la crème*. If desired, serve
with fresh cream, or a sauce made by heating
4 tablespoons redcurrant jelly and 4 tablespoons
water until jelly melts, and stirring in 2 to 4 tablespoons Kirsch or cognac.

29

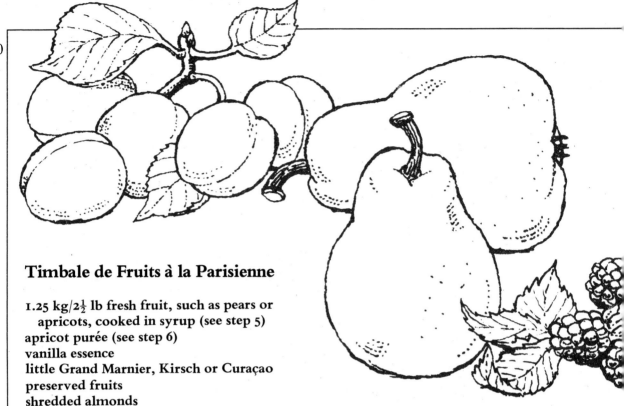

Timbale de Fruits à la Parisienne

1.25 kg/2½ lb fresh fruit, such as pears or apricots, cooked in syrup (see step 5)
apricot purée (see step 6)
vanilla essence
little Grand Marnier, Kirsch or Curaçao
preserved fruits
shredded almonds

BRIOCHE
450 g/1 lb plain flour
15 g/½ oz dried yeast
salt
lukewarm water
4 eggs
2-4 level tablespoons sugar
butter

1. To make a yeast sponge: sift 100 g/4 oz flour into a small mixing bowl and make a well in the centre. Sprinkle yeast and a pinch of salt into 4 tablespoons lukewarm water; after a few minutes, stir well. Strain yeast mixture into the centre of the flour. Make into a soft dough. Roll this in a little flour to make a ball and cut it across the top with a sharp knife. Place 'sponge' in just enough warm water to cover it while you are preparing the dough – about 15 minutes. Keep the water warm but not hot over a saucepan, and the 'sponge' will swell to two or three times its original volume.

2. To make the dough: sift 350 g/12 oz flour into a mixing bowl and make a well in the centre. Add eggs to well, and mix in the flour gradually to make a soft dough. When well mixed, turn dough out on a lightly floured board and knead it until the dough becomes smooth and elastic and no longer sticks to your fingers. Then mix in the sugar, a pinch of salt and 100-175 g/4-6 oz slightly softened butter. When these are well incorporated, drain the 'sponge', place it in the centre of the other dough, and mix the two doughs lightly. Place the dough in a floured bowl, cover it and let it stand in the natural heat of the kitchen for about 3 hours, by which time it should have doubled its original volume. Knock the dough back to its original size, and set it in a cool place until the next day, knocking it down again if it rises too much. It may be kept for 24 hours in this way so long as it is not allowed to rise too much.

3. To make a large brioche: butter a soufflé mould 20 to 25 cm/8 to 10 inches in diameter and tie a strong band of buttered greaseproof paper round the outside to make a high mould. Half-fill the mould with *brioche* dough and set it in a warm place to rise. When the dough has risen to the top of the mould, put it in a moderately hot oven (190°C, 375°F, Gas Mark 5) to bake for 30 to 40 minutes, until brown.

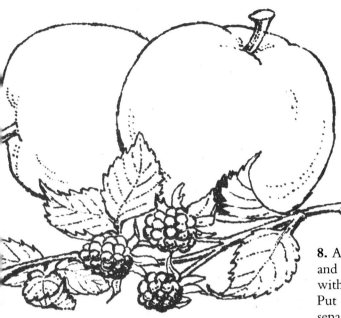

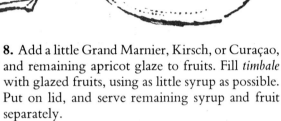

8. Add a little Grand Marnier, Kirsch, or Curaçao, and remaining apricot glaze to fruits. Fill *timbale* with glazed fruits, using as little syrup as possible. Put on lid, and serve remaining syrup and fruit separately.

4. When *brioche* is one day old, cut the top off and reserve for lid. With a sharp knife cut around the inside of the *brioche*, 1 cm/½ inch in from the sides and down to within 2.5 cm/1 inch of the bottom. Pass the knife round once or twice to make sure that the inside dough is free from the crust. Then insert the knife through the side of the crust 2.5 cm/1 inch from the bottom of the *brioche* and move it gently from right to left to sever the centre piece entirely, making the hole as small as possible. Lift out the soft centre part, leaving a case or crust of *brioche* – the '*timbale*'.

5. To prepare fruit for filling: peel and dice fresh fruit and cook until tender in a syrup of 2 tablespoons sugar and 150 ml/¼ pint water flavoured with vanilla essence.

6. To make apricot glaze: Sieve or liquidise 6–8 canned apricot halves (or 150 ml/¼ pint apricot jam). Mix purée in a small saucepan with some of the fruit syrup (see step 5), flavour with vanilla essence and/or a little liqueur (Grand Marnier, Kirsch or Curaçao), and boil quickly until reduced to a thick syrup or jelly.

7. Brush this hot syrup over *timbale*, glazing well both inside and out. Decorate top edge with preserved fruits and shredded almonds, while syrup is still sticky.

Blackberry and Apple Sponge

1 kg/2 lb apples
225 g/8 oz blackberries, hulled and washed
4-6 level tablespoons castor sugar
cream or Vanilla Custard Sauce (see page 91)

SPONGE
75 g/3 oz butter
75 g/3 oz castor sugar
2 eggs, beaten
100 g/4 oz self-raising flour
25 g/1 oz cornflour

1. Peel, core and slice the apples into a pie dish, and add hulled and washed blackberries and sugar.

2. To make sponge: cream butter and sugar until light and fluffy. Add eggs one at a time, adding a little flour with the second egg. Fold in the remaining flour and cornflour.

3. Spread sponge mixture over the fruit. Bake in a moderately hot oven (190°C, 375°F, Gas Mark 5) for 30 to 40 minutes. Sprinkle with a little castor sugar, and serve hot with cream or Vanilla Custard Sauce.

Apple Bread Pudding

32

about 14 slices fresh bread, cut medium thick
100 g/4 oz butter, softened
675 g/1½ lb tart apples
finely grated rind and juice of 1 lemon
finely grated rind and juice of ½ orange
50 g/2 oz Demerara sugar
2 level tablespoons raisins
generous pinch of ground cloves
¼ level teaspoon ground cinnamon
450 ml/¾ pint Vanilla Custard Sauce (see page 91)

1. Remove crusts from the bread and butter each slice generously on one side. Cut 3 or 4 small rounds from each slice with a cutter. Cut bread trimmings (not crusts) into small dice.

2. Butter a 1.25-litre/2-pint rectangular baking dish generously and line base and sides completely with some of the bread rounds, buttered sides inwards.

3. Peel, core and cut apples into small chunks. Toss them thoroughly with lemon and orange juice and finely grated lemon and orange rind, sugar, raisins and spices.

4. Pack half the apple mixture into the bread-lined baking dish and dot with a level tablespoon of butter.

5. Scatter surface with diced bread and fill to the top with remaining apple mixture. Press down slightly and dot with another tablespoon of butter. Cover surface entirely with overlapping bread rounds, buttered sides uppermost.

6. Cover pudding loosely with a sheet of foil and bake in a moderately hot oven (190°C, 375°F, Gas Mark 5) for 30 to 40 minutes, removing foil for last 10 minutes of cooking time.

7. Serve warm with Vanilla Custard Sauce (or whipped cream flavoured with a little rum).

Zuppa Inglese

900 ml/1½ pints milk
½ teaspoon vanilla essence
¼ level teaspoon ground cinnamon
1 strip lemon rind
pinch of salt
4-6 tablespoons sugar
1 level tablespoon cornflour
8 egg yolks
6-8 tablespoons rum
grated rind and juice of ½ orange
4 tablespoons Kirsch
finely grated chocolate

SPONGE CAKE
6 egg yolks
225 g/8 oz sugar
2 tablespoons lemon juice or water
grated rind of ½ lemon
generous pinch of salt
75 g/3 oz plain flour, sifted 4 times
25 g/1 oz cornflour
6 egg whites

1. To make sponge cake: beat egg yolks, sugar, lemon juice or water, lemon rind and salt until light and fluffy (5 minutes at high mixer speed). Sift flour and cornflour, and mix into egg yolk mixture a little at a time. Whisk egg whites until soft peaks form, and fold gently into egg yolk mixture. Divide mixture into two unbuttered 21-cm/8½-inch cake tins. Cut through mixture gently several times to break up any larger air bubbles. Bake in a moderate oven (180°C, 350°F, Gas Mark 4) for 25 to 30 minutes. Test by denting with finger; if the cake is done, the dent will spring back. Invert cakes on wire trays. When cool, loosen edges and remove from tins.

2. Combine milk, vanilla essence, cinnamon, lemon rind and salt in a saucepan, and bring just to boiling point. Remove from heat.

3. Mix sugar and cornflour together in the top of a double saucepan. Add egg yolks and blend well. Gradually stir in the scalded milk, and cook over hot water, stirring constantly, until mixture is smooth and thick. Remove from heat. Cool. Remove lemon peel.

4. At least 2 hours before serving: place 1 layer of cake in a serving dish, sprinkle with rum and orange juice, and cover with about two-thirds of the cooled custard mixture. Top with second cake, sprinkle with Kirsch and pour over remaining sauce. Chill.

5. Just before serving, remove from refrigerator and sprinkle with finely grated chocolate and orange rind.

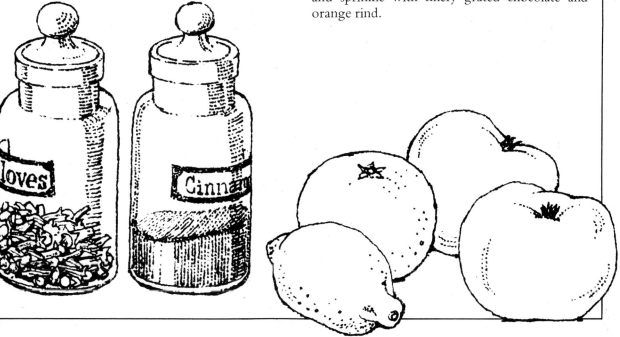

34

Simple Rice Pudding

8 level tablespoons rice
butter
2–4 level tablespoons sugar
salt
nutmeg or other flavouring
750 ml/1¼ pints milk
150 ml/¼ pint double cream
2 level tablespoons finely shredded or
   chopped suet or butter
sultanas (optional)

1. Wash the rice, and put it in a well-buttered pie dish with the sugar, salt, and a little grated nutmeg or other flavouring. Pour in milk and double cream, and sprinkle the finely shredded or chopped suet over the top.

2. Bake the pudding in a moderate oven (180°C, 350°F, Gas Mark 4) for 2 to 3 hours, until the rice is quite soft. The slower it is cooked, the softer and creamier it will be. Sultanas may also be added if desired.

Old English Rice Pudding

6 level tablespoons rice
150 ml/¼ pint water
900 ml/1½ pints milk
pinch of salt
grated lemon rind
150 ml/¼ pint double cream
sugar
2 eggs, separated
butter

1. Wash the rice and put it in a saucepan with the water. Bring to the boil and cook until water is absorbed.

2. Add the milk, salt and a little grated lemon rind. Reduce heat and simmer slowly for about 15 minutes, until the rice is thoroughly cooked, stirring occasionally with a wooden spoon.

3. When ready, remove the saucepan from the heat, and when slightly cooled, stir in cream, 2 tablespoons sugar and egg yolks.

4. Whisk egg whites until stiff and fold them lightly into mixture. Pour the mixture into a well-buttered pie dish, and bake in a moderate oven (180°C, 350°F, Gas Mark 4) until nicely browned. Sprinkle with sugar.

Rice à la Royale

75 g/3 oz rice
300 ml/½ pint milk
4-6 tablespoons sugar
pears poached in syrup
chopped pistachio nuts or shredded almonds

CUSTARD
300 ml/½ pint milk
½ level teaspoon cornflour
4-6 level tablespoons sugar
4 egg yolks
vanilla essence
2 sheets leaf gelatine, or 7 g/¼ oz powdered
    gelatine
150 ml/¼ pint double cream
2-3 tablespoons Kirsch

1. Place rice, milk and sugar in a saucepan, bring to the boil and simmer until rice is tender. Cool.

2. To make custard: Scald milk and remove from heat. Mix cornflour and sugar together in top of a double saucepan. Add egg yolks and blend well. Gradually stir in scalded milk and cook over hot water, stirring constantly, until mixture is smooth and thick. Flavour to taste with vanilla essence, strain and divide into two equal parts.

3. If using leaf gelatine, soak in water for 10 minutes. Drain and dissolve in any water clinging to the gelatine, over a gentle heat. If using powdered gelatine, sprinkle over 2 tablespoons water and allow to soften. Stir gelatine over hot water until completely dissolved and clear. Add to one part of the custard, reserving remainder to use as a sauce.

4. When the rice is cool, add custard containing gelatine along with 2 or 3 tablespoons double cream, and additional sugar if desired. Mix lightly and spoon into a china or glass serving dish.

5. Drain poached pears, pat them dry of syrup and arrange on top of rice. Add remaining cream to remaining custard, flavour with Kirsch and pour it around pears and over pudding. Sprinkle pears with chopped pistachio nuts or shredded almonds. Serve very cold.

Cold Soufflés

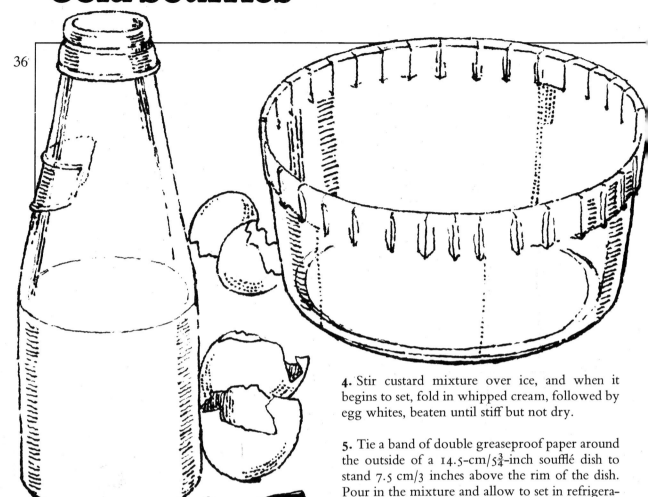

4. Stir custard mixture over ice, and when it begins to set, fold in whipped cream, followed by egg whites, beaten until stiff but not dry.

5. Tie a band of double greaseproof paper around the outside of a 14.5-cm/5¾-inch soufflé dish to stand 7.5 cm/3 inches above the rim of the dish. Pour in the mixture and allow to set in refrigerator. Remove paper carefully before serving.

Basic Cold Soufflé

300 ml/½ pint milk
2.5-cm/1-inch vanilla pod
3 egg yolks
3 level tablespoons sugar
1 level tablespoon powdered gelatine
3 tablespoons water
150 ml/¼ pint double cream, whipped
4 egg whites

1. Heat milk with vanilla pod. Remove pod and keep milk hot.

2. Whisk egg yolks and sugar until thick and lemon-coloured. Add hot milk and cook over hot water without allowing mixture to boil.

3. Dissolve gelatine in water and add to custard, strain and cool.

Cold Lemon Soufflé

6 egg yolks
175 g/6 oz castor sugar
juice of 2 large lemons
grated rind of 1 lemon
6 egg whites, stiffly beaten
25 g/1 oz powdered gelatine
150 ml/¼ pint water
½ jar redcurrant jelly
2 tablespoons Kirsch or lemon juice
1 tablespoon water

1. Beat egg yolks thoroughly with sugar, lemon juice and grated lemon rind. Transfer mixture to the top of a double saucepan and whisk over hot water, until mixture thickens.

2. Remove from the heat and allow to cool

slightly. Then fold in the stiffly beaten egg whites.

3. Dissolve gelatine in water and fold into egg mixture. Pour the mixture into a serving bowl and chill.

4. Whisk redcurrant jelly with a little Kirsch, or lemon juice, and water, and serve separately.

Chocolate Soufflé Glacé
Illustrated on page 48

1 medium-sized orange
1 level tablespoon instant coffee
150 g/5 oz bitter chocolate
15 g/½ oz powdered gelatine
6 eggs
100 g/4 oz castor sugar
300 ml/½ pint double cream
1-2 tablespoons brandy, rum or liqueur
   (optional)
coarsely grated dark bitter chocolate and
   whipped cream, to decorate

1. Tie a band of double greaseproof paper around the outside of a 14.5-cm/5¾-inch soufflé dish (measured across the top), to stand 7.5 cm/3 inches above the rim of the dish. Select two bowls, a large one for beating the eggs and a smaller one for melting chocolate. Find a saucepan over which both bowls will fit securely. Fill saucepan half full with water. Fit each bowl in position over the pan and check that base does not touch water. Put water on to heat gently.

2. Scrub the orange clean and dry it thoroughly with a cloth. Finely grate rind into the smaller bowl. Squeeze juice and strain it into the same bowl. Add instant coffee, dissolved in 3 tablespoons boiling water, and chocolate broken into small pieces. Put aside.

3. In a small bowl or cup, sprinkle gelatine over 4 tablespoons cold water and put aside to soften until needed. Break eggs into the large bowl and add sugar.

4. When water in saucepan comes to the boil, reduce heat to a bare simmer. Fit bowl containing

eggs and sugar over pan, and whisk vigorously until mixture is light and bulky, and leaves a trail on the surface when beaters are lifted.

5. Remove bowl and in its place put the smaller bowl containing chocolate mixture. Heat gently until chocolate has completely melted. Meanwhile, continue to whisk egg mixture until barely lukewarm.

6. When chocolate has melted, remove from heat. Remove saucepan of water from heat as well. Stand bowl (or cup) containing softened gelatine in the hot water and stir until completely dissolved. Remove. Whisk chocolate mixture lightly to ensure it is quite free of lumps.

7. When chocolate mixture and dissolved gelatine are both just warm, blend them together thoroughly.

8. Pour cream into a bowl and whisk carefully until it is just thick enough to leave a barely perceptible trail on the surface. (If you have been using an electric mixer so far, this operation may be safer done with a hand whisk to avoid over-whipping cream.)

9. Quickly and lightly fold chocolate gelatine mixture into cream. Then, before mixture has had a chance to start setting, fold it into the cooled whisked egg mixture, together with brandy, rum or liqueur, if used. Stop folding as soon as you have got rid of chocolate 'streaks' in mixture.

10. Stand prepared soufflé dish on a plate. Pour in soufflé mixture, taking care not to dislodge or crumple paper collar. Leave it to firm slightly for 15 to 20 minutes before transferring dish to the refrigerator. Chill soufflé for 2 to 3 hours until firmly set.

11. Just before serving, peel off paper collar. Press coarsely grated bitter chocolate around exposed sides of soufflé and decorate top with grated chocolate and piped whipped cream.

38

Amaretti Soufflé Glacé

½ level teaspoon powdered gelatine
4 egg yolks
100 g/4 oz granulated sugar
300 ml/½ pint milk
3-4 tablespoons Amaretti liqueur
few drops of vanilla essence
300 ml/½ pint double cream
6 small Italian macaroons (amaretti),
   crushed

1. Turn refrigerator down to lowest temperature, (i.e. highest setting).

2. Select 6 individual soufflé dishes about 6 cm/2½ inches in diameter and tie double-thickness collars of greaseproof paper around them to come 2.5 cm/1 inch above the rim.

3. In a small cup, sprinkle gelatine over 1 tablespoon cold water and leave to soften.

4. In a bowl, beat egg yolks with sugar until thick and light.

5. Pour milk into the top of a double saucepan and bring to the boil over direct heat. Then whisk into egg mixture in a thin stream.

6. Return mixture to double saucepan and stir over gently simmering water until it coats back of spoon, taking care not to let custard boil, or egg yolks will curdle. Cool slightly.

7. Dissolve softened gelatine by standing cup in hot water and stirring until liquid is clear. Blend into the cool custard, together with *Amaretti* liqueur and a few drops of vanilla essence, to taste.

8. Whip double cream until soft peaks form and fold into custard.

9. Divide mixture between prepared soufflé dishes. It should come well above the rim of each dish.

10. Freeze for about 5 hours, or until very firm. Then transfer to the main compartment of the refrigerator for about 1 hour before serving.

11. To serve: sprinkle top of each iced soufflé with finely crushed macaroons, patting the crumbs in lightly to make them stick. Carefully peel off paper collars and serve immediately.

Soufflé Glacé Praliné 'East Arms'

90 g/3½ oz sugar
4 egg yolks, well beaten
100 g/4 oz loaf sugar
100 g/4 oz chopped almonds
350 ml/12 fl oz double cream, whipped
6 egg whites, stiffly beaten
crystallised violets (optional)

1. Boil 4 tablespoons water and the sugar in the top of a double saucepan until sugar is dissolved. Allow to cool and add beaten egg yolks. Whisk over simmering water until mixture is thick and light. Allow to cool.

2. Boil loaf sugar and 4 tablespoons water until sugar is caramel-coloured. Stir in almonds and pour into an oiled baking tin. When cool, crush with a rolling pin.

3. Mix custard mixture, whipped cream and crushed almond mixture until smooth, and then carefully fold in stiffly beaten egg whites. Pour soufflé mixture into 2 0.75-litre/1-pint soufflé dishes with a band of double greaseproof paper tied around the outside. Allow to set in refrigerator for 5 to 6 hours. Remove the bands of paper and decorate with crystallised violets if desired.

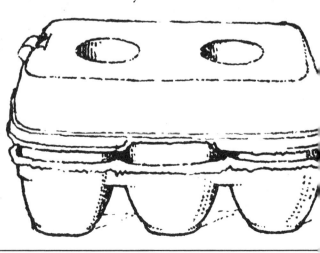

Soufflé Glacé au Cointreau

400 ml/14 fl oz whipped cream
4-6 level tablespoons chopped crystallised
fruits
Cointreau

CRÈME PÂTISSIÈRE
8 egg yolks
225 g/8 oz castor sugar
400 ml/14 fl oz milk
1 vanilla pod

MERINGUE ITALIENNE
8 egg whites
450 g/1 lb sugar
6-8 tablespoons water

1. To make Crème Pâtissière: beat egg yolks
and sugar together until mixture is lemon-
coloured. Then add milk and vanilla pod, and
mix thoroughly. Place mixture in the top of a
double saucepan and cook over water, stirring
constantly, until smooth and thick. Remove from
heat and discard vanilla pod. Sieve and allow to
cool.

2. To make Meringue Italienne: beat egg
whites until stiff but not dry. Then melt the sugar
and water and cook until you can pull it to a fine
thread with a spoon. Allow to cool. Pour syrup
over egg whites gradually, beating well as you
pour.

3. Add Crème Pâtissière to the cold meringue,
together with whipped cream, some crystallised
fruits, and Cointreau, to taste.

4. Tie a band of double greaseproof paper around
the outside of a 15 to 18-cm/6 to 7-inch porcelain
soufflé dish to stand 7.5 cm/3 inches above the rim
of the dish. Pour the mixture into the soufflé dish,
allowing it to come above the rim of the dish (it
will be held in place by the paper). Chill in the
refrigerator, and just before serving, remove the
band of paper. The *soufflé glacé*, higher than the
dish, will give the appearance of a raised soufflé.

Mocha Bavarois

40 g/1½ oz bitter chocolate
450 ml/¾ pint milk
6 egg yolks
175 g/6 oz castor sugar
2 level tablespoons instant coffee
2 tablespoons orange liqueur
15 g/½ oz powdered gelatine
4 tablespoons very cold milk
300 ml/½ pint double cream
flavourless cooking oil for brushing

TO DECORATE
2 level tablespoons freshly roasted coffee
 beans
1 tablespoon orange liqueur
whipped cream

1. Break chocolate into small pieces. Pour milk into the top of a double saucepan, scald over direct heat. Add chocolate and stir until dissolved.

2. Beat egg yolks with sugar until fluffy and lemon-coloured. Gradually add scalded chocolate milk mixture, beating constantly.

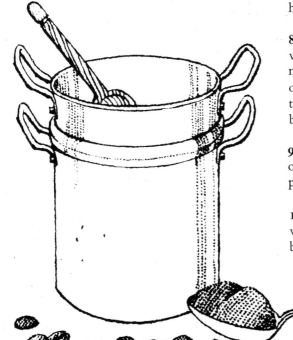

3. Dissolve instant coffee in 3 tablespoons boiling water. Stir into milk mixture. Pour back into top of double saucepan and cook over lightly simmering water, stirring constantly for about 20 minutes until mixture coats back of spoon. Take care not to let it boil, or egg yolks will curdle.

4. As soon as custard has thickened, plunge pan into cold water to arrest cooking process and cool custard slightly. Stir in liqueur.

5. Soften gelatine in 3 tablespoons cold water. Then put basin in a pan of hot water (the bottom half of the double saucepan is the most convenient), and stir until gelatine has completely dissolved and liquid is clear. Stir into the cooling custard. Leave until cold and just on the point of setting.

6. Add cold milk to double cream and whisk until floppy. Ideally, it should have the same consistency as the cold custard, so that the two can be combined with the minimum of folding. Fold cream into cold custard.

7. Brush a 1.25-litre/2-pint mould with oil. Pour in *bavarois* mixture and chill until set; allow 2 hours at least.

8. To unmould bavarois: dip mould in hot water **for 2 to 3 seconds only** to loosen cream – not too long, or cream will begin to melt. Turn out carefully on to a serving dish, and return to the bottom of the refrigerator until an hour before serving.

9. To decorate bavarois: soak coffee beans in orange liqueur for at least 30 minutes, longer if possible. Drain them and chop coarsely.

10. Just before serving, decorate *bavarois* with whipped cream and sprinkle with chopped coffee beans.

Chocolate Rum Mousse

175 g/6 oz milk chocolate
5 eggs, separated
1 teaspoon vanilla essence
1-2 level teaspoons instant coffee
1 tablespoon hot water
300 ml/½ pint double cream
2 tablespoons rum

1. Melt chocolate in the top of a double saucepan over hot but not boiling water. Remove from heat and allow to cool.

2. Beat egg yolks lightly and then beat them gradually into the melted chocolate. Flavour to taste with vanilla essence and instant coffee dissolved in hot water.

3. Whip cream until thick, stir in rum and fold into the chocolate mixture.

4. Beat egg whites until stiff and fold into the mixture.

5. Pour mixture into a serving dish. Chill for at least 2 hours.

Soufflé Glacé aux Fraises
Illustrated on page 47

225 g/8 oz granulated sugar
6 egg whites
450 ml/¾ pint strawberry purée
300 ml/½ pint double cream, whipped
juice of lemon or lime
icing sugar

1. Boil the sugar with 450 ml/¾ pint water until it reaches the soft ball stage (115°C/240°F).

Note: Test sugar syrup from time to time while cooking by dropping a little syrup into a small bowl of iced water. When you can pick it out and roll it into a tiny ball the syrup is ready to use.

2. Beat egg whites very stiff and carefully fold in the slightly sugar cooled syrup. Chill in the freezer compartment of your refrigerator or in the freezer, until it reaches the mushy stage. (**Note:** You'll find it necessary to stir egg white and syrup mixture from time to time to keep it from separating.) Then remove from the freezer and gently fold in the strawberry purée and the stiffly whipped cream. Add lemon or lime juice and mix well.

3. Tie a band of double greaseproof paper around the outside of a 0.75-litre/1-pint soufflé dish, to stand 5 cm/2 inches above the rim of the dish. Pour the soufflé mixture into the dish and freeze for about 2 hours.

4. Just before serving, remove the band of paper and dust soufflé liberally with icing sugar.

Chocolate Mould

50 g/2 oz plain chocolate
450 ml/¾ pint milk
7 g/¼ oz powdered gelatine
25-50 g/1-2 oz sugar
2 egg yolks
¼ teaspoon vanilla essence
whipped cream

1. Break the chocolate into small pieces and put it in a saucepan with 150 ml/¼ pint milk. Dissolve chocolate slowly, until smooth.

2. Then remove saucepan from heat, and add the remaining milk, gelatine, sugar and egg yolks. Stir again over heat until the mixture is hot, and the gelatine has dissolved. **Do not allow the mixture to boil.**

3. Strain mixture into a bowl and add vanilla essence. Allow to cool slightly, then pour mixture into a wet mould and set aside until firm.

4. When ready to serve, invert mould on to a serving dish. Serve with whipped cream.

Hot Soufflés

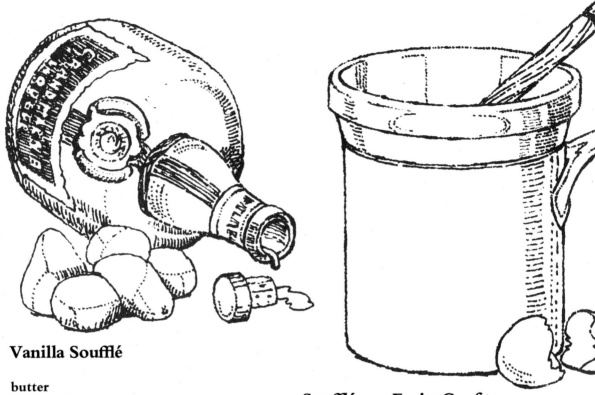

Vanilla Soufflé

butter
3 level tablespoons flour
300 ml/½ pint hot milk
pinch of salt
5 egg yolks
sugar
½ teaspoon vanilla essence
6 egg whites

1. Melt 4 level tablespoons butter in the top of a double saucepan. Stir in the flour and cook until well blended. Add hot milk and salt, stirring constantly, and cook until smooth and thick. Continue cooking and stirring for a few more minutes. Let sauce cool slightly.

2. Beat egg yolks well with 4 tablespoons sugar and vanilla essence, and mix well with sauce. Beat egg whites until they are stiff but not dry, and fold gently into the sauce mixture.

3. Pour the mixture into a buttered and lightly sugared 1.5-litre/2½-pint soufflé dish, and bake in a moderate oven (180°C, 350°F, Gas Mark 4) for 35 to 45 minutes, until the soufflé is puffed and golden. Serve at once.

Soufflé aux Fruits Confits

6 level tablespoons crystallised fruits,
    coarsely chopped
2 tablespoons cognac
4 egg yolks
2 level tablespoons flour
4 level tablespoons sugar
300 ml/½ pint double cream
½ teaspoon vanilla essence
4 tablespoons Grand Marnier
5 egg whites
pinch of salt
butter
whipped cream

1. Soak coarsely chopped crystallised fruits in cognac for at least 2 hours.

2. Beat egg yolks, flour and sugar together in the top of a double saucepan. Add the cream. Place over hot water and cook, stirring constantly, until thick and smooth. Do not allow to come to the boil. Stir in vanilla essence and Grand Marnier. Allow to cool, stirring occasionally.

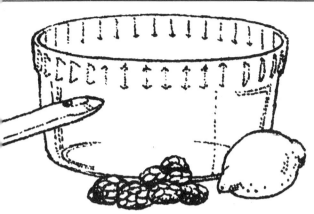

3. Beat the egg whites and salt until stiff but not dry, and fold into the cooled mixture. Pour half the mixture into a buttered 1.25-litre/2-pint soufflé dish. Scatter cognac-soaked fruits over soufflé mixture and then cover with remaining mixture. Bake in a moderate oven (180°C, 350°F, Gas Mark 4) for 35 minutes, or until soufflé is well puffed and golden. Serve immediately with whipped cream.

Raspberry Lemon Soufflé

350 g/12 oz frozen raspberries
6 tablespoons Kirsch or Framboise liqueur
50 g/2 oz castor sugar
5 egg yolks
100 g/4 oz icing sugar, sifted
3 level tablespoons flour, sifted
450 ml/$\frac{3}{4}$ pint milk
$\frac{1}{2}$ level teaspoon finely grated lemon rind
3 tablespoons lemon juice
1 level tablespoon butter
50 g/2 oz stale sponge cake
6 egg whites
pinch of salt

1. Place frozen raspberries in a wide dish. Sprinkle with Kirsch or Framboise liqueur and castor sugar, and leave to defrost completely, about 2 hours, turning occasionally.

2. Grease a 1.5-litre/2$\frac{1}{2}$-pint soufflé dish with butter, paying particular attention to the top rim, and dust with granulated sugar, shaking out excess. Set soufflé dish in a deep baking tin and put aside until needed.

3. Preheat oven to moderately hot (200°C, 400°F, Gas Mark 6).

4. Put egg yolks in the top of a double saucepan, add sifted icing sugar and beat with a wire whisk until light and well blended. Add sifted flour, beating constantly until mixture is smooth.

5. In another pan, bring milk to the boil. Remove from heat and add to egg yolk mixture in a thin stream, beating vigorously.

6. Place the egg mixture over a pan of simmering water and cook, stirring constantly, for 7 to 10 minutes, until custard is thick and smooth. Then remove from heat and beat in finely grated lemon rind, lemon juice and butter. Pour custard into a large bowl and allow to cool to lukewarm, stirring occasionally to prevent a skin forming on top.

7. Drain raspberries thoroughly in a sieve, reserving juices.

8. Cut sponge cake into neat, 5-mm/$\frac{1}{4}$-inch dice. Toss lightly with raspberry juices until thoroughly saturated but not crumbly. Any juice which has not been absorbed by the sponge cake may be beaten into the cooling custard.

9. Place egg whites in a large, spotlessly clean, dry bowl. Add a pinch of salt and whisk until stiff but not dry.

10. Fold egg whites into lukewarm custard, using a spatula or a large metal spoon, folding in as quickly and as lightly as possible. Finally, fold in the raspberries and soaked sponge, taking care not to knock any air out of the mixture.

11. Spoon mixture into prepared soufflé dish. Pour 2.5 cm/1 inch of boiling water into the baking tin and gently bring back to the boil over a low heat.

12. As soon as water bubbles, transfer to the oven. Immediately reduce oven temperature to moderate (180°C, 350°F, Gas Mark 4) and bake soufflé for 45 to 50 minutes until well puffed and just set in the centre – this is a very creamy, moist soufflé. Serve immediately.

Chocolate Soufflé

44

65 g/2½ oz chocolate
150 ml/¼ pint milk
4-6 level tablespoons castor sugar
3 egg yolks
vanilla essence
1 level tablespoon cornflour
4 level tablespoons double cream
4 egg whites

1. Break chocolate into small pieces and place in a saucepan with half the milk. Cook gently, stirring occasionally until chocolate is melted.

2. Combine sugar, egg yolks and vanilla essence, to taste, in a mixing bowl, and work them together with a wooden spoon until they are of a creamy consistency. Mix remaining milk with cornflour and add it gradually to the egg mixture, together with the chocolate. Pour into a saucepan and cook until almost boiling. Remove from heat, add cream and cook for a few minutes, stirring occasionally.

3. Beat egg whites until stiff and fold them into chocolate mixture. Pour into a well-buttered 1-litre/1½-pint soufflé dish and bake in a moderate oven (180°C, 350°F, Gas Mark 4) for 30 to 40 minutes, until well risen and firm to the touch. Should the soufflé become too brown, put a piece of paper over the top. Sprinkle with a little sugar just before serving.

Chocolate Rum Soufflé

50 g/2 oz plain chocolate, cut in small pieces
300 ml/½ pint hot milk
4 level tablespoons butter
3 level tablespoons flour
100 g/4 oz sugar
4 egg yolks
pinch of salt
1-2 tablespoons Jamaica rum
5 egg whites, stiffly beaten
whipped cream

1. Melt chocolate in the milk in the top of a double saucepan and beat until smooth and hot. Do not

allow it to come to the boil. Melt butter in a saucepan and blend in flour and sugar. Add chocolate mixture and stir over a low heat until the mixture starts to boil. Remove from heat.

2. Beat egg yolks and stir in 2 tablespoons of the hot chocolate mixture. Then pour the egg yolks into the chocolate mixture. Add salt and Jamaica rum, and beat over a low heat until mixture thickens slightly.

3. Remove from heat, and when cool, fold in stiffly beaten egg whites. Pour mixture into a 20-cm/8-inch soufflé dish. Place dish in a baking tin two-thirds full of boiling water and cook in moderate oven (160°C, 325°F, Gas Mark 3) for 45 minutes, or until soufflé is puffed and golden. Serve immediately with whipped cream.

Apricot Soufflé

4 level tablespoons butter
3 level tablespoons flour
300 ml/½ pint hot milk
pinch of salt
3 egg yolks
100 g/4 oz sugar
4 tablespoons Kirsch
300 ml/½ pint puréed apricots, cooked in
   syrup
4 egg whites

1. Melt butter in the top of a double saucepan. Stir in the flour and cook until well blended. Add hot milk and salt stirring constantly and cook the sauce until smooth and thick. Continue cooking and stirring a little longer, then cool slightly.

2. Beat egg yolks well with sugar and combine with the sauce. Flavour with 2 tablespoons Kirsch and add puréed apricots, to which you have added remaining Kirsch. Let the mixture get cold, then fold in egg whites, beaten until they are stiff but not dry.

3. Place mixture into a lightly buttered and sugared 14.5-cm/5¾-inch soufflé dish. Cook in a moderate oven (180°C, 350°F, Gas Mark 4) for 30 to 35 minutes, until cooked.

Fresh Fruit Sorbets

Pineapple Water Ice (see page 16)

Soufflé Glacé aux Fraises (see page 41)

Chocolate Soufflé Glacé (see page 37)   **Biscuit Tortoni (see page 20)**

Tangerine Sorbet with Lychees (see page 17)

Normandy Soufflé

2 ripe apples
butter
2 level tablespoons sugar
2 ripe pears
lemon juice
2 tablespoons Calvados or cognac
5 egg whites

CRÈME PÂTISSIÈRE
4 egg yolks
100 g/4 oz sugar
2 level tablespoons sifted flour
300 ml/½ pint milk
½ teaspoon vanilla essence

1. To make Crème Pâtissière: beat egg yolks
and sugar together until mixture is lemon-
coloured. Stir in flour, then add milk and vanilla
essence, and mix thoroughly. Place mixture in top
of a double saucepan and cook over water, stirring
constantly, until smooth and thick. Remove from
heat and sieve. Allow to cool.

2. Peel, core and slice apples. Add 1 tablespoon
butter and sugar, and simmer over a gentle heat
until soft. Peel and core pears. Mash pears and
cooked apples, drain off excess liquid if necessary,
and flavour to taste with sugar, lemon juice and
Calvados or cognac.

3. Whisk egg whites until stiff and fold into
Crème Pâtissière. Place half the custard in a well-
buttered 1.25-litre/2-pint soufflé dish. Cover with
a layer of fruit purée and top with remaining
custard mixture. Bake in a moderate oven (180°C,
350°F, Gas Mark 4) for 40 minutes. Serve at once.

Soufflé Puddings

8 tablespoons softened butter
100 g/4 oz icing sugar
100 g/4 oz plain flour, sifted
400 ml/14 fl oz milk, boiled
½-1 teaspoon vanilla essence
5 egg yolks
6 egg whites

SABAYON SAUCE
4 egg yolks
100 g/4 oz sugar
175 ml/6 fl oz Marsala
1 tablespoon cognac

1. Work butter into a *pommade* in a mixing bowl.
Add icing sugar and sifted flour, beating well
between each addition. Dilute with hot milk
flavoured with vanilla essence.

2. Cook over a high heat, stirring continuously,
until mixture dries out and leaves the side of the
pan (like a *pâte à choux*).

3. Remove from heat; thicken with egg yolks,
one by one, then carefully fold in the beaten egg
whites. Pour into well-buttered individual soufflé
dishes and place in a baking tin half filled with hot
water. Cook in a moderate oven (180°C, 350°F,
Gas Mark 4) for 40 to 45 minutes, until puddings
are cooked. Serve with Sabayon Sauce.

4. To make Sabayon Sauce: whisk egg yolks
and sugar until yellow and frothy in the top of a
double saucepan. Add the Marsala; place over hot
water and cook until thick and foamy, stirring
constantly. Stir in cognac and chill.

Variations

Orange Curaçao Soufflé Puddings
Kümmel Soufflé Puddings
Benedictine Soufflé Puddings

Make puddings as above, but flavour with the
liqueur of your choice. Serve with Sabayon
Sauce flavoured with the same liqueur used for the
puddings instead of Marsala and cognac as in
above recipe.

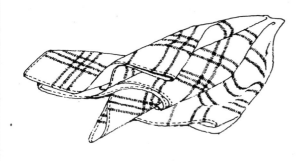

Batters, Crêpes and Fritters

50

Basic French Crêpes (for Sweet Filling)

100 g/4 oz plain flour
½ level teaspoon salt
2 level tablespoons sugar
2 eggs
450 ml/¾ pint milk
butter or oil

1. Sift flour, salt and sugar into a mixing bowl. Beat eggs and add them to dry ingredients. Mix in milk and 2 tablespoons melted butter or oil and beat until smooth. Strain through a fine sieve and leave batter to stand for at least 2 hours before cooking the *crêpes*. Batter should be as thin as cream. Add a little water if too thick.

2. Place about 2 tablespoons batter into a heated and buttered pan, swirling pan to allow batter to cover entire surface thinly. Brush a piece of butter around edge of hot pan with the point of a knife and cook over a medium heat until just golden but not brown (about 1 minute each side). Repeat until all *crêpes* are cooked, stacking them on a plate as they are ready.

Batter I

(To use for fritters, croquettes or batter-fried meats, fish or poultry)

100 g/4 oz plain flour
pinch of salt
150 ml/¼ pint warm water or milk
1 tablespoon oil or melted butter
2-3 egg whites

Sift flour and salt into a mixing bowl, and make a well in the centre. Gradually pour water or milk into the well, beating with a wooden spoon to make batter smooth and free from lumps. Add oil or melted butter and beat again for a few minutes. Whisk egg whites to a stiff froth and fold them lightly into the batter. Use immediately and cook as for Basic French Crêpes (see above).

Batter II

(**Beer Batter**: excellent for prawns, shrimps and other seafood)

225 g/8 oz plain flour
pinch of salt
2 eggs, well beaten
2 tablespoons oil or melted butter
1 tablespoon brandy
300 ml/½ pint pale ale

Sift flour and salt into a mixing bowl, and make a well in the centre. Stir beaten eggs into the well and then gradually beat in the other ingredients until batter is perfectly smooth. Cover the bowl and let batter stand for at least 6 hours in a very cool place before using. Cook as for Basic French Crêpes (see above).

Swedish Pancakes

100 g/4 oz plain flour
1 level tablespoon sugar
½ level teaspoon salt
2 egg yolks
450 ml/¾ pint warm milk
2 tablespoons melted butter
2 egg whites, stiffly beaten
preserved lingonberries or cranberries
beaten butter (see step 3)

1. Sift flour, sugar and salt into mixing bowl. Beat egg yolks and add them to dry ingredients. Combine warm milk and melted butter and gradually beat in avoiding any lumps. Strain through a fine sieve and leave batter to stand for at least 2 hours.

2. Before cooking beat again, and fold in stiffly beaten egg whites. Bake on either a greased griddle, a large iron frying pan, or a special Swedish *plattar* pan with indentations for pancakes. Pour in enough batter to make pancakes about 7.5 cm/3 inches in diameter. Cook as for Basic French Crêpes (see above).

3. Serve with preserved lingonberries and beaten butter. (Soften fresh butter and beat it in electric mixer on low speed until smooth. Then beat on highest speed until butter is fluffy and a delicate light yellow colour – 8 to 10 minutes. If you store it in refrigerator, allow to soften again at room temperature before using.)

Pfannkuchen (German Pancakes)

3 eggs, beaten
300 ml/½ pint milk
generous pinch of salt
1 level tablespoon sugar
75 g/3 oz plain flour
butter
strawberry jam, cooked apples or Chocolate Sauce (see page 90)
cinnamon-flavoured sugar

1. Beat eggs, milk, salt, sugar and flour together and stand for 30 minutes.

2. Brush thick-bottomed 25-cm/10-inch frying pan with butter. Pour in 5 to 6 tablespoons batter at a time tilting pan to make batter spread to form large, flat pancake. Cook over medium heat until batter bubbles. Turn and cook other side. Stack on plate in heated oven.

3. Coat each pancake with butter and strawberry jam, cooked apples or Chocolate Sauce, and roll up. Cut each pancake in half. Sprinkle with cinnamon sugar.

Crêpes des Oliviers

51

150 g/5 oz plain flour
100 g/4 oz sugar
200 ml/7 fl oz warm milk
4 eggs, beaten
100 g/4 oz butter
grated rind and juice of 2 oranges
Grand Marnier

1. Combine flour and 2 tablespoons sugar in a mixing bowl, and gradually beat in warm milk, beaten eggs and melted butter. Add finely grated rind of 1 orange to flavour the *crêpes* batter and allow to stand for 2 hours before using.

2. Make a syrup with remaining sugar, grated rind of remaining orange and juice of 2 oranges. Flavour to taste with Grand Marnier.

3. Make pancakes in usual way and fold in four. Place on a well-buttered ovenproof dish and heat through in the syrup.

Crêpes aux Marrons Glacés

½ quantity Basic French Crêpes (see page 50)
150 ml/¼ pint double cream
vanilla essence
icing sugar
8 marrons glacés, chopped

1. Make about 12 *crêpes*, transferring them to a warm plate as you cook them.

2. Whip cream, flavoured to taste with vanilla essence and icing sugar, adding a little iced water to make mixture lighter. Fold in chopped *marrons glacés* with syrup. Fill *crêpes* with this mixture and roll up. Dust with icing sugar.

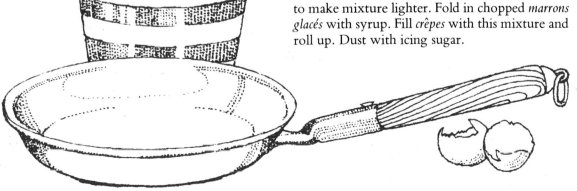

52

Crêpes aux Fruits

½ quantity Basic French Crêpes (see page 50)
3 eating apples, peeled, cored and diced
butter
juice of ½ lemon
4 level tablespoons apricot jam
4 level tablespoons chopped almonds
150 ml/¼ pint whipped cream
2-3 tablespoons Calvados
crushed macaroons
sugar

1. Make about 12 *crêpes*, transferring them to a warm plate as you cook them.

2. Cook diced apples in 3 tablespoons butter and lemon juice until tender. Stir in apricot jam and chopped almonds. Then fold in whipped cream flavoured with Calvados.

3. Cover *crêpes* with apple mixture, fold in four and place them in a buttered flameproof dish. Sprinkle with crushed macaroons and sugar, and place under a preheated grill for a minute or two to glaze.

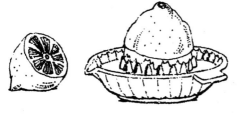

Crêpes au Kümmel

225 g/8 oz plain flour
75 g/3 oz icing sugar
4 eggs
3 egg yolks
vanilla essence
600 ml/1 pint milk
8 level tablespoons double cream
2 level tablespoons butter
3 tablespoons Kümmel
finely crushed macaroons

1. Sift flour and icing sugar into a mixing bowl, then beat in eggs and egg yolks one at a time until mixture is thick and lemon-coloured.

2. Add vanilla essence to milk, and heat. Combine with double cream and beat gradually into batter mixture. Add butter, which you have cooked until it is light brown in colour and Kümmel (cognac or rum may be substituted). Strain through a fine sieve and let stand for 1 to 2 hours.

3. Cook as for Basic French Crêpes (see page 50). Place *crêpes* one on top of the other as they are cooked, sprinkling each with icing sugar and finely crushed macaroons.

Crêpes aux Mandarines

½ quantity Basic French Crêpes (see page 50)
grated rind of 1 mandarin orange
2-4 tablespoons Curaçao

BEATEN MANDARIN BUTTER
225 g/8 oz fresh butter
juice of 1 mandarin orange
little grated mandarin orange rind
2-4 tablespoons Curaçao

1. Make *crêpes* adding grated mandarin rind and Curaçao, to taste. Place in an ovenproof dish and keep hot in the oven. At the table, place a spoonful of Beaten Mandarin Butter on each *crêpe*, fold in four and serve immediately.

2. To make beaten Mandarin Butter: soften fresh butter and beat it at low speed in electric mixer until smooth. Then add mandarin juice, a little grated mandarin rind and Curaçao. Beat at high speed until butter is fluffy and a delicate light yellow in colour – 8 to 10 minutes.

Apple Fritters

4 ripe apples
sugar
lemon or orange juice
rum or cognac
1 quantity Batter I or II (see page 50)
fat or oil for deep-frying

1. Peel, core and chop the apples. Sprinkle them with sugar and a little lemon or orange juice, and rum or cognac, to taste. Let them stand for a few minutes, and then mix them with Batter I or II.

2. Place a spoonful of the mixture at a time in hot fat or oil and fry until puffed and golden brown in colour. Do not make fritters too large or they will not cook through. Test the first one before lifting the others from the fat. Sprinkle with sugar and serve immediately.

American Apple Fritters

2 level tablespoons butter
2 level tablespoons sugar
2 eggs, separated
175 g/6 oz plain flour, sifted
1-2 tablespoons milk
1 level teaspoon baking powder
pinch of salt
3 ripe apples, peeled, cored and finely
  chopped
fat or oil for deep-frying
icing sugar

1. Cream butter and sugar until smooth. Beat egg yolks into mixture, then gradually add the sifted flour and milk, beating well. Add baking powder and salt, then fold in finely chopped apple. Beat egg whites until stiff and fold them gently into the mixture.

2. Form the mixture into small balls the size of a walnut. Drop them into hot fat or oil, and fry until golden. Drain, sprinkle with icing sugar and serve immediately.

Fresh Peach Fritters

4 ripe peaches
sugar
Maraschino or Kirsch
macaroon crumbs
1 quantity Batter I or II (see page 50)
fat for frying
lemon wedges

1. Peel and stone peaches, and cut into quarters. Sprinkle the pieces with sugar and a few drops of

Maraschino or Kirsch, and toss in macaroon crumbs. Allow to stand for a few minutes.

2. Dip the coated peaches in Batter I or II, lifting each one out with a skewer and dropping it into a saucepan of hot fat.

3. Fry fritters, turning them from time to time, until golden brown on all sides. Lift fritters out of fat with a skewer or perforated spoon and dry on sugared paper in a moderate oven (160°C, 325°F, Gas Mark 3). Continue until all are cooked. Serve with additional sugar and lemon wedges.

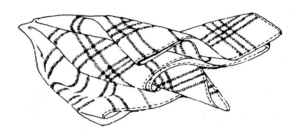

Pear Fritters

4 ripe pears
sugar
white wine
Kirsch
macaroon or cake crumbs
1 quantity Batter I or II (see page 50)
fat or oil for deep-frying
lemon wedges

1. Peel and core pears, and cut into quarters or eighths. Sprinkle slices with sugar and marinate in dry white wine with a little Kirsch for at least 15 minutes.

2. Toss slices in macaroon or cake crumbs, and dip in batter, lifting each piece out with a skewer.

3. Fry fritters in hot fat or oil, turning them from time to time, until golden brown on all sides. Lift fritters out of fat with a skewer or perforated spoon and dry on sugared paper in a moderate oven (160°C, 325°F, Gas Mark 3). Continue until all are cooked. Serve with additional sugar and lemon wedges.

Steamed Puddings

54

Basic Steamed or Boiled Sponge Pudding

butter
3 level tablespoons jam
3 level tablespoons castor sugar
1 egg, well beaten
75 g/3 oz plain flour
150 ml/¼ pint milk
1 level teaspoon baking powder
pinch of salt
Vanilla Custard Sauce or Ginger Sauce
    (see page 91)

1. Butter a 1.25-litre/2-pint pudding basin and coat bottom with jam.

2. Cream 2 tablespoons butter with sugar in a mixing bowl, add beaten egg and half the flour. Beat well and then add the milk and remaining flour. The mixture should have the consistency of a thick batter that will just drop from the spoon. Beat again, and finally add baking powder and salt, to taste.

3. Pour the mixture into the prepared basin, cover with buttered paper then secure tightly with a double thickness of foil. Steam for 45 to 60 minutes, until well risen and firm to the touch. When ready, turn out and serve quickly. Serve with Vanilla Custard Sauce or Ginger Sauce.

Baroness Pudding

225 g/8 oz plain flour
½ level teaspoon salt
1 level teaspoon baking powder
25 g/1 oz castor sugar
100 g/4 oz suet, chopped
100 g/4 oz sultanas
150 ml/¼ pint milk
butter
Apricot Sauce or Vanilla Custard Sauce
    (see page 91)

1. Sift flour, salt and baking powder into a mixing bowl, add sugar, finely chopped suet and sultanas.

2. Mix dry ingredients together thoroughly, make a well in the centre and gradually pour in enough milk to make a soft dough.

3. Pour the mixture into a well-buttered 1.25-litre/2-pint basin which you have decorated with a few sultanas. Cover with buttered paper then secure tightly with a double thickness of foil. Steam steadily for 3 hours. Serve with Apricot Sauce or Vanilla Custard Sauce.

Rich Steamed or Boiled Sponge Pudding

butter
4-6 level tablespoons tart jam or warm
    syrup, honey or treacle
225 g/8 oz plain flour
2 level teaspoons baking powder
100 g/4 oz butter
100 g/4 oz castor sugar
2 eggs
about 150 ml/¼ pint milk

FLAVOURINGS
vanilla essence
grated lemon rind
mixed ground spice, cinnamon or ginger
50 g/2 oz sultanas or raisins
Vanilla Custard Sauce (see page 91)

1. Butter a 1.25-litre/2-pint pudding basin and spread jam, syrup, honey or treacle over the bottom and about a quarter of the way up sides.

2. Sift flour and baking powder into a mixing bowl.

3. Rub in butter with your fingertips until mixture resembles fine breadcrumbs. Stir in sugar and make a well in the centre.

4. Beat eggs lightly. Pour them into the well, together with enough milk to make a batter with a good dropping consistency. Beat vigorously with a wooden spoon until smoothly blended.

5. Beat in chosen flavouring.

6. Pour batter into prepared basin. Cover surface with a disc of buttered greaseproof paper, then cover basin tightly with a double thickness of foil, or tie on a pudding cloth.

7. Steam or boil pudding for $1\frac{1}{2}$ to 2 hours until well risen and firm to the touch.

8. To serve: turn pudding out on to a hot serving dish and serve immediately with a Vanilla Custard Sauce.

Chelsea Pudding

100 g/4 oz suet
100 g/4 oz breadcrumbs
100 g/4 oz plain flour
salt
1 level teaspoon baking powder
100 g/4 oz currants
100 g/4 oz raisins
250 ml/8 fl oz treacle or molasses, slightly
    warmed
250 ml/8 fl oz milk
butter
Vanilla Custard Sauce (see page 91)

1. Chop suet finely and mix with breadcrumbs, flour, salt and baking powder. Mix well together with the tips of the fingers, then add the currants and raisins.

2. Make a well in the centre, stir in slightly warmed treacle, then gradually add milk, beating all together. Pour mixture into a well-buttered 1.25-litre/2-pint pudding basin, or copper mould, cover with buttered paper, then secure tightly with a double thickness of foil. Steam steadily for 3 hours. When ready, turn out and serve with Vanilla Custard Sauce.

Steamed Gingerbread Pudding

100 g/4 oz suet
100 g/4 oz plain flour, sifted
1 level teaspoon ground ginger
$\frac{1}{2}$ level teaspoon ground cinnamon
1 level teaspoon baking powder
pinch of salt
250 ml/8 fl oz treacle or molasses
1 egg, well beaten
250 ml/8 fl oz milk
butter
Vanilla Custard Sauce (see page 91)

1. Chop suet finely and mix it in a bowl with sifted flour, ground ginger and cinnamon, and baking powder, adding salt to taste.

2. Make a well in the centre, pour in the treacle and well-beaten egg, and gradually mix in the dry ingredients, adding the milk slowly as you mix. Beat for a minute and pour the mixture into a well-buttered 1.25-litre/2-pint pudding basin, or copper mould. Cover with buttered paper and secure tightly with a double thickness of foil. Steam steadily for 2 to 3 hours, until well risen and firm to the touch. When ready, turn out and serve with Vanilla Custard Sauce.

56

Chocolate Bread Pudding

75 g/3 oz semi-sweet chocolate
50 g/2 oz butter
150 ml/¼ pint milk
50 g/2 oz castor sugar
2 eggs, separated
150 g/5 oz fresh white breadcrumbs
pinch of ground cinnamon
vanilla essence
Chocolate Sauce or Vanilla Custard Sauce
  (see pages 90, 91)

1. Dissolve chocolate with butter in the top of a double saucepan. Add milk and simmer gently. Sprinkle sugar over the top, add egg yolks and half the breadcrumbs, and mix well. Stir in remaining breadcrumbs, cinnamon and vanilla essence, to taste.

2. Whisk egg whites to a stiff froth. Fold them into mixture at the last moment, and then pour mixture into a well-buttered 1.25-litre/2-pint pudding basin. Cover with buttered paper and secure tightly with a double thickness of foil. Steam for 1 to 1½ hours, until the pudding is well risen and feels firm to the touch. Serve with Chocolate Sauce or Vanilla Custard Sauce.

Steamed Apricot Pudding

50 g/2 oz butter
50 g/2 oz castor sugar
50 g/2 oz plain flour
2 eggs
4-6 canned apricot halves
pinch of ground cinnamon
grated rind and juice of ½ lemon
¼ level teaspoon baking powder
300 ml/½ pint Apricot Sauce (see page 91)

1. Cream butter and sugar in a bowl until light and fluffy. Gradually add the flour and eggs. Beat well until light and frothy.

2. Drain the apricot halves and cut them in small pieces. Add them to the mixture with the cinnamon, lemon rind and lemon juice, and last of all the baking powder. Mix well and pour into a

well-buttered pudding basin. Cover with buttered paper and secure tightly with a double thickness of foil.

3. Steam for 1 to 1½ hours, until the pudding is well risen and firm to the touch.

4. When ready, turn out and strain the Apricot Sauce over pudding.

Steamed Cherry Pudding

225 g/8 oz fresh cherries
75 g/3 oz brown breadcrumbs
65 g/2½ oz castor sugar
grated rind of ½ lemon
150 ml/¼ pint double cream
2 egg yolks, beaten
2 egg whites
butter
juice of ½ lemon
100 ml/4 fl oz water
red food colouring (optional)

1. Combine breadcrumbs, 40 g/1½ oz castor sugar and grated lemon rind in a mixing bowl.

2. Wash, pick and stone the cherries, and add three-quarters of them to breadcrumb mixture.

3. Scald cream and pour over the crumbs and fruit. Stir in beaten egg yolks.

4. Beat whites until stiff and fold into mixture.

5. Pour the mixture into a well-buttered 1.25-litre/2-pint mould or basin. Cover with a piece of buttered paper then secure tightly with a double thickness of foil. Steam slowly and steadily for about 1½ hours, or until pudding is well risen and firm to the touch.

6. Combine remaining cherries, lemon juice, water and 25 g/1 oz sugar in a saucepan. Bring to the boil, reduce heat and simmer gently for 15 minutes. Tint sauce with red food colouring if necessary. Invert the pudding carefully on a hot dish, pour the sauce around it and serve immediately.

Traditional English Christmas Pudding

A home-made Christmas pudding can never be a last-minute preparation. First of all, the raw mixture has to stand overnight before being cooked, and then the pudding must be left to mature in a cool, dry place for 3 to 4 months, preferably longer.

350 g/12 oz sultanas
350 g/12 oz raisins
350 g/12 oz currants
350 g/12 oz shredded suet
225 g/8 oz fresh white breadcrumbs
225 g/8 oz soft dark brown sugar
100 g/4 oz self-raising flour, sifted
100 g/4 oz chopped mixed peel
1 level teaspoon mixed spice
$\frac{1}{2}$ level teaspoon freshly grated nutmeg
$\frac{1}{4}$ level teaspoon salt
2 level tablespoons treacle or golden syrup
1 level teaspoon finely grated orange rind
1 level teaspoon finely grated lemon rind
4 tablespoons fresh orange juice
4 tablespoons lemon juice
4 large eggs, lightly beaten
150 ml/$\frac{1}{4}$ pint stout
8 tablespoons brandy

TO SERVE
sprig of holly
sifted icing sugar
brandy
Brandy Sauce or Brandy Butter
  (see page 90)

1. Pick over dried fruit and if necessary, wash and dry thoroughly on a cloth.

2. In a large porcelain or earthenware bowl, assemble first eleven ingredients and toss together until thoroughly mixed. Make a large well in the centre.

3. In another, smaller bowl, blend treacle or syrup thoroughly with grated orange and lemon rinds. Blend in orange and lemon juice gradually, and when mixture is smooth again, beat in lightly beaten eggs, stout and brandy.

4. Pour this mixture into dry ingredients and stir vigorously with a large wooden spoon until well blended.

5. Cover bowl with a damp cloth and leave overnight in a cool place to allow flavours to develop.

6. The following day, start by preparing your pudding basins. Grease two 1.4-litre/2$\frac{1}{2}$-pint pudding basins with butter and line bottoms with circles of buttered greaseproof paper.

7. Divide pudding mixture evenly between prepared basins, levelling off tops.

8. Cover top of each pudding with another circle of buttered greaseproof paper, then cover basins with pudding cloths and tie down with string.

9. Steam puddings for 3 hours, taking care not to let water underneath evaporate. Allow to cool before storing in a cool, dry cupboard.

10. On the day you wish to serve a pudding, steam it slowly for 2 hours until thoroughly reheated.

11. To serve: turn pudding out on to a heated serving dish. Decorate with holly and a sifting of icing sugar, and flame with brandy at the table. (To avoid an anti-climax it is best to heat the brandy in a large metal ladle or spoon and set it alight *before* pouring it over the pudding.) Serve with Brandy Sauce, Brandy Butter or whatever accompaniment is traditional in your family.

Tarts,
Flans and Pastry

58

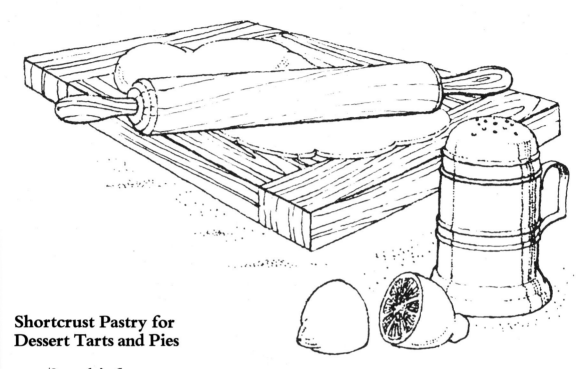

Shortcrust Pastry for
Dessert Tarts and Pies

225 g/8 oz plain flour
1 tablespoon icing sugar
squeeze of lemon juice
pinch of salt
100 g/4 oz butter, diced
½ teaspoon vanilla essence
iced water

1. Sift flour and sugar into a mixing bowl. Add lemon juice, salt, butter and vanilla essence, cover well with the flour and rub together lightly with the tips of the fingers until the mixture resembles fine breadcrumbs. Whilst rubbing in, keep lifting the flour well up in the bowl, so that air may mix with it and the butter is not made too soft.

2. When pastry is thoroughly mixed, make a well in the centre and gradually add 1-2 tablespoons cold water, mixing with one hand or a knife. Do not add too much water, or pastry will be tough instead of short.

3. Sprinkle the pastry board with flour, turn the dough on it and knead lightly with the hands until dough is smooth. Flour a rolling pin, press down pastry and then with sharp quick strokes roll pastry on one side only to the thickness required. Roll pastry lightly and try to press equally with both hands. Never allow pastry to stick to the board, but lift occasionally on the rolling pin and dust some flour underneath. If dough has stuck to the board, scrape it off carefully with a knife before beginning to roll again. Always sprinkle flour over board and pastry using a flour sifter to make it finer and lighter, using as little flour as possible for this, as too much tends to make the pastry hard. If the rolling pin sticks to the pastry, dust with a little flour and brush it off again lightly with a small brush kept for this purpose.

4. To bake pastry: a fairly hot oven is required for pastry. If it is not hot enough the butter will melt and run out before the starch grains in the flour have had time to burst and absorb it. If the oven is too hot, however, the pastry will burn before it has risen properly. When baking pastry, open and close the door as gently as possible and never more often than is absolutely necessary. If pastry becomes too brown before it has cooked sufficiently, cover it over with a piece of foil or a double sheet of greaseproof paper that has been lightly sprinkled with water. If pastry is not to be used at once when taken from the oven, allow it to cool slowly in the warm kitchen. Light pastry tends to become heavy when cooled too quickly.

To bake 'blind'
Line a 20 or 23-cm/8 or 9-inch flan ring or tin with pastry, fluting the edges if necessary and chill. Prick bottom with a fork, cover bottom of pastry with a piece of waxed paper or foil and cover with dried beans. Bake in a hot oven (230°C, 450°F, Gas Mark 8) for about 15 minutes, just long enough to set the crust without browning it. Remove beans, paper or foil and allow to cool. Fill with desired filling and bake in a moderately hot oven (190°C, 375°F, Gas Mark 5) until cooked. The beans can be reserved in a storage jar and used again.

To bake pastry case only
Bake 'blind' as above for 15 minutes, remove beans and foil. Reduce oven temperature to moderately hot (190°C, 375°F, Gas Mark 5) and bake for 10 to 15 minutes. If crust becomes too brown at edges, cover rim with a little crumpled foil.

Rich Biscuit Crust
A richer pastry for dessert tarts and pies can be made in the same way, using 150–175 g/5–6 oz butter and adding 1 egg yolk, beaten with a little water for mixing.

Rich Shortcrust Pastry

225 g/8 oz plain flour
½ level teaspoon salt
1 level tablespoon icing sugar
150 g/5 oz butter
1 teaspoon lemon juice
1 egg yolk, beaten with 1 tablespoon water
1-2 tablespoons water

1. Sift flour, salt and icing sugar into a mixing bowl. Dice slightly softened butter and add to flour mixture. Using pastry blender or two knives scissor fashion, cut in butter until blend begins to crumble. Then rub in butter with the tips of fingers until mixture resembles fine breadcrumbs. Do this very gently and lightly or the mixture will become greasy and heavy. Add lemon juice, beaten egg yolk and water mixture gradually, all the time tossing gently from bottom of bowl with a fork. Add water and mix into a soft dough.

2. Shape dough lightly into 2 flattened rounds, place in a polythene bag and put in refrigerator for at least an hour, or overnight, to ripen and become firm.

3. If chilled dough is too firm to handle, leave it at room temperature until it softens slightly. Pat one ball of dough on a floured board with a lightly floured rolling pin to flatten and shape it. Then roll from the centre to edges until pastry is 3 mm/⅛ inch thick and 5 cm/2 inches larger in diameter than pie dish. Fold in half and lift into position over dish. To prevent shrinkage, ease pastry gently into dish without stretching.

Use in the following ways:
Two-crust Pie: Fill with fruit, moisten edge, cover with remaining pastry and press edges together to seal. Trim off excess pastry, press edge with fork or crimp with fingers. Cut slits in top for the steam to escape. Bake in a moderately hot oven (200°C, 400°F, Gas Mark 6) for 30 minutes, or until crust is brown and fruit is tender.

One-crust Pie: Using scissors, trim pastry 1 cm/½ inch beyond edge of dish. Fold edge under and crimp with fingers. Prick the base with a fork and cover bottom of pastry with a piece of waxed paper or foil. Fill with dried beans and bake in a hot oven (220°C, 450°F, Gas Mark 7) for about 15 minutes, just long enough to set the crust without browning it. Remove beans, paper or foil and allow to cool. Fill with uncooked filling and bake in a moderately hot oven (190°C, 375°F, Gas Mark 5) until cooked.

Flan case: Line flan ring or dish with pastry and prick bottom and sides well with fork. Bake 'blind' (see above) in a hot oven (230°C, 450°F, Gas Mark 8) for 15 minutes. Remove beans and foil then reduce oven temperature to moderately hot (190°C, 375°F, Gas Mark 5) and bake for a further 10 to 15 minutes.

60

Fingertip Pastry for Tarts and Flans

225 g/8 oz plain flour
pinch of salt
2 level tablespoons icing sugar
150 g/5 oz butter, finely diced
1 egg yolk
4 tablespoons cold water

1. Sift flour, salt and sugar into a mixing bowl. Rub in butter with the tips of fingers until mixture resembles fine breadcrumbs. Do this very gently and lightly, or mixture will become greasy and heavy.

2. Beat egg yolk and cold water and sprinkle over dough working in lightly with your fingers. Shape moist dough lightly into a flattened round. Place in a polythene bag and leave in refrigerator for at least 1 hour to 'ripen'.

3. If chilled dough is too firm for handling, allow to stand at room temperature until it softens slightly. Then, turn it on to a floured board and roll out as required. Press into a 20 to 23-cm/8 to 9-inch flan ring, pie dish or individual patty tins with your fingers and prick with a fork. Cover bottom of pastry with a piece of waxed paper or foil. Fill with dried beans and bake in a hot oven (230°C, 450°F, Gas Mark 8) for about 15 minutes. Reduce oven temperature to moderate (180°C, 350°F, Gas Mark 4) and bake for 30 minutes. If crust becomes too brown at edges, cover with a little crumpled foil.

Pineapple Tart

Illustrated on page 65

1 (23-cm/9-inch) shortcrust pastry case, unbaked (see page 58)
fresh pineapple sliced into thin rings
glacé cherries

FRENCH PASTRY CREAM
100 g/4 oz sugar
3 level tablespoons cornflour
450 ml/¾ pint milk
5 egg yolks
½-1 teaspoon vanilla essence
2 teaspoons Kirsch

APRICOT GLAZE
6-8 level tablespoons apricot jam
3 tablespoons water
1-2 tablespoons rum, brandy or Kirsch (optional)

1. To bake prepared pastry case: bake 'blind' in a hot oven (230°C, 450°F, Gas Mark 8) for 15 minutes. Reduce oven temperature to moderate (180°C, 350°F, Gas Mark 4) and bake for 30 minutes. If crust becomes too brown at edges, cover with a little crumpled foil.

2. To make French pastry cream: combine sugar and cornflour in the top of a double saucepan. Stir in milk and cook over direct heat, stirring all the time, until mixture comes to the boil. Boil for 1 minute. Beat yolks slightly, add a little hot milk mixture and pour back into milk and sugar mixture, stirring. Cook over hot but not boiling water, stirring until thickened – 5 to 10 minutes. Strain and cool. Add vanilla essence and Kirsch. Cover with waxed paper and chill thoroughly.

3. To make apricot glaze: heat apricot jam and water in a small saucepan, stirring constantly, until mixture melts. Strain, and stir in rum, brandy or Kirsch if desired. Keep warm over hot water.

4. To assemble tart: half fill baked pastry case with French Pastry Cream and arrange thin slices of fresh pineapple in overlapping rows on top. Coat with golden-coloured apricot glaze. Decorate tart with glacé cherries. Serve chilled.

Individual Apple Tarts

Illustrated on page 65

4 individual pastry cases, baked
675 g/1½ lb eating apples, peeled, cored and thinly sliced
melted butter

CRÈME PÂTISSIÈRE
450 ml/¾ pint milk
5-cm/2-inch piece vanilla pod, split
5 egg yolks
100 g/4 oz castor sugar
2 level tablespoons plain flour
1 level tablespoon cornflour
1 level tablespoon butter
few drops of vanilla essence

APRICOT GLAZE
6 level tablespoons apricot jam
3 tablespoons water
1 tablespoon rum, brandy or Kirsch

1. To make crème pâtissière: pour milk into a medium-sized pan and add vanilla pod, split to give out maximum flavour. Bring to boiling point over a low heat. Cover pan and put aside to infuse until needed. In a bowl, whisk egg yolks with sugar until thick and light. Gradually whisk in flour and cornflour. Take out vanilla pod. Gradually pour milk into egg yolk mixture, beating with the whisk until well blended. Pour mixture back into pan. Bring to the boil over a moderate heat, stirring constantly. Then simmer for 3 minutes longer, beating vigorously with a wooden spoon to disperse lumps. (These lumps invariably form, but you will find that they are easy to beat out as the cream thickens.) Remove pan from heat. Beat in butter and continue to beat for a minute or two longer to cool the pastry cream slightly before adding vanilla essence. Pass cream through a sieve if necessary. Put it in a bowl and cover with a sheet of lightly buttered grease-proof paper to prevent a skin forming on top. Allow the *crème pâtissière* to become quite cool.

2. To make apricot glaze: heat apricot jam and water in a small saucepan, stirring constantly, until mixture melts. Strain. Stir in rum, brandy or Kirsch. Keep warm over hot water.

3. Half fill baked pastry cases with *crème pâtissière*. Cover with overlapping rings of thinly sliced eating apples. Brush with melted butter and bake in a hot oven (230°C, 450°F, Gas Mark 8) for 5 minutes. If apples do not brown sufficiently at edges to be attractive, put under grill for a minute or two. Cool tarts then brush with apricot glaze.

62

French Raspberry Tart

1 (23-cm/9-inch) shortcrust pastry case,
   unbaked (see page 58)
fresh raspberries, to cover

FRENCH PASTRY CREAM
100 g/4 oz sugar
3 level tablespoons cornflour
450 ml/¾ pint milk
5 egg yolks
½–1 teaspoon vanilla essence
2 teaspoons Kirsch

RASPBERRY GLAZE
6–8 level tablespoons raspberry jam
3 tablespoons water
1–2 tablespoons Kirsch

1. To bake prepared pastry case: bake 'blind' in a hot oven (230°C, 450°F, Gas Mark 8) for 15 minutes. Reduce oven temperature to moderate (180°C, 350°F, Gas Mark 4) and bake for 30 minutes. If crust becomes too brown at edges, cover with a little crumpled foil.

2. To make French pastry cream: combine sugar and cornflour in the top of a double saucepan. Stir in milk and cook over direct heat, stirring all the time, until mixture comes to the boil. Boil for 1 minute. Beat yolks slightly, add a little hot milk mixture and pour back into milk and sugar mixture, stirring. Cook over hot but not boiling water, stirring until thickened – 5 to 10 minutes. Strain and cool. Add vanilla essence and Kirsch. Cover with waxed paper and refrigerate until well chilled.

3. To make raspberry glaze: heat raspberry jam and water in a small saucepan, stirring constantly, until mixture melts. Strain and stir in Kirsch. Keep warm.

4. To assemble tart: half-fill baked pastry case with French pastry cream and arrange raspberries in circles on top. Coat with glaze. Serve chilled.

Apple Pie with Cheese Apples

8 tart eating apples
225 g/8 oz rich shortcrust pastry (see
   page 59)
50 g/2 oz granulated sugar
50 g/2 oz dark brown sugar
1 level tablespoon flour
½ teaspoon grated nutmeg
grated rind of 1 orange
grated rind of 1 lemon
75 g/3 oz chopped raisins and sultanas
2 tablespoons orange juice

CHEESE APPLES
225 g/8 oz processed cheese
angelica or clove 'stalks'
paprika

1. Peel and core apples. Cut each into 8 to 10 slices, depending on size.

2. Line a deep 23-cm/9-inch pie dish with two-thirds of the shortcrust pastry.

3. Combine granulated sugar, dark brown sugar, flour and nutmeg. Sprinkle a little into pastry case. Add grated rinds to remaining sugar mixture.

4. Arrange sliced apples, sultanas and raisins in pastry case, sprinkling each layer with some of the sugar mixture. Pour over the orange juice. Fit remaining pastry over apple layers, pressing the edges together or fluting them. Cut several slits in the top of the pastry crust to release steam. Bake in a hot oven (220°C, 425°F, Gas Mark 7) for 40 to 45 minutes until tender.

5. To make cheese apples: roll processed cheese into little balls approximately 2.5 cm/1 inch in diameter. Press thumb in top to form indentation for angelica or clove 'stalk'. Dust cheek of 'apple' with paprika for 'blush'.

6. Serve pie warm with tiny cheese 'apples' placed around outside of pie crust.

Little Christmas Tarts

Illustrated on page 68

**individual shortcrust pastry cases, baked
(see page 58)**

VANILLA CREAM
175 g/6 oz sugar
3 tablespoons flour
2½ level tablespoons cornflour
450 ml/¾ pint milk
6 egg yolks
6 level tablespoons butter
vanilla essence
Grand Marnier

APRICOT GLAZE
6-8 level tablespoons apricot jam
3 tablespoons water
**1 tablespoon rum, brandy or Kirsch
(optional)**

FRUITS
**whole strawberries, grapes, mandarin
segments, pear slices, pineapple slices,
peach slices, banana slices, whole cherries,
apricot halves, etc.**

1. To make vanilla cream: combine sugar, flour and cornflour in the top of a double saucepan. Stir in milk and cook over direct heat, stirring all the time, until the mixture comes to the boil. Boil for 1 minute. Beat egg yolks lightly and add a little hot milk mixture, then pour into saucepan with milk and sugar mixture, stirring constantly. Cook over hot but not boiling water stirring for 5 minutes. Strain and allow to cool slightly. Mix with butter and flavour to taste with vanilla essence and Grand Marnier.

2. To make apricot glaze: heat apricot jam and water in a small saucepan, stirring constantly, until mixture melts. Strain and stir in rum, brandy or Kirsch if desired. Keep warm over hot water until ready to use.

3. Place a spoonful of vanilla cream in the bottom of each individual pastry case. Arrange fruits of your choice on top of vanilla cream and glaze with golden coloured apricot glaze.

Easy Fruit Bande

63

**canned pear halves, sliced into 6 or 8,
according to size**
canned sliced peaches
small canned pineapple rings, halved
canned orange segments
canned mandarin segments
fresh black grapes
crisp dessert apples
lemon juice

WHIPPED HONEY CREAM
2 level tablespoons clear honey
1 tablespoon orange juice
1-2 teaspoons lemon juice
150 ml/¼ pint double cream
¼ level teaspoon ground cinnamon

1. Drain canned fruits thoroughly, reserving syrup, and slice or halve as directed. Wash and halve grapes.

2. Peel and core some of the apples and slice into rings 8 mm/⅓ inch thick. Toss rings in lemon juice until thoroughly coated to prevent discoloration. As a contrast, use apples with bright red skins, and prepare as before.

3. Arrange prepared fruits in closely overlapping rows on a long shallow serving dish, taking colour and texture into account when deciding on the order. Sprinkle with some of the syrup from canned fruit or a little castor sugar, or spoon over a glaze made with syrup from cans thickened with arrowroot (2 level teaspoons arrowroot to 150 ml/¼ pint syrup). Serve with whipped honey cream.

4. To make whipped honey cream: put honey in a small bowl or jug and gradually stir in orange and lemon juice with a teaspoon. Whip cream until slightly thickened. Gradually whisk in honey mixture, and continue to whisk until cream is of a soft floppy consistency. Whisk in cinnamon to taste.

64

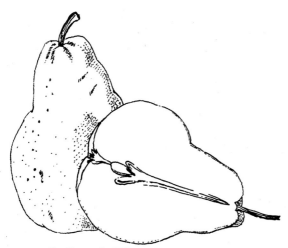

French Peach Flan
Illustrated opposite

1 (20-23-cm/8-9-inch) fingertip pastry case,
  baked (see page 60)
fresh peaches

FRENCH PASTRY CREAM
100 g/4 oz sugar
3 level tablespoons cornflour
450 ml/¾ pint milk
5 egg yolks
½-1 teaspoon vanilla essence
2 teaspoons Kirsch

APRICOT GLAZE
6-8 level tablespoons apricot jam
3 tablespoons water
1 tablespoon rum, brandy or Kirsch
  (optional)

1. To make French pastry cream: combine
sugar and cornflour in the top of a double saucepan. Stir in milk and cook over direct heat,
stirring all the time, until mixture comes to the
boil. Boil for 1 minute. Beat yolks slightly, add a
little hot milk mixture and pour back into milk
and sugar mixture, stirring. Cook over hot but
not boiling water, stirring until thickened – 5 to
10 minutes. Strain and cool. Add vanilla essence
and Kirsch. Cover with waxed paper and refrigerate until well chilled.

2. To make apricot glaze: heat apricot jam and
water in a small saucepan, stirring constantly, until

mixture melts. Strain and stir in rum, brandy or
Kirsch if desired. Keep warm over hot water.

3. To assemble flan: half fill baked pastry case
with French pastry cream and arrange halved
fresh peaches on top. Coat with golden-coloured
apricot glaze.

Grape Tart Pâtissière
Illustrated on page 67

1 (23-cm/9-inch) shortcrust pastry case,
  unbaked (see page 58)
225 g/8 oz green grapes
225 g/8 oz black grapes
French Pastry Cream (see above)

APRICOT GLAZE
6-8 level tablespoons apricot jam
3 tablespoons water
1-2 tablespoons Kirsch

DECORATION (optional)
1 egg white
1 small bunch black grapes
castor sugar

1. To bake prepared pastry case: bake 'blind'
in a hot oven (230°C, 450°F, Gas Mark 8) for 15
minutes. Reduce oven temperature to moderate
(180°C, 350°F, Gas Mark 4) and bake for 30
minutes. If crust becomes too brown at edges,
cover with a little crumpled foil.

2. Peel and deseed grapes.

3. To assemble tart: half fill baked pastry case
with French pastry cream. Arrange grapes decoratively on top. Coat with apricot glaze.

4. To make apricot glaze: add 3 tablespoons
water to apricot jam and heat, stirring constantly,
until melted. Flavour to taste with Kirsch.

5. To decorate: lightly beat the egg white. Dip
bunch of black grapes into the egg white, holding
it by the stalk. Drain slightly and then roll gently
in castor sugar. Leave to dry and then place in
centre of flan.

Pineapple Tart (see page 60); Chocolate Pear Flan (see page 69);
Individual Apple Tarts (see page 61); French Peach Flan (see page 64);
Orange and Almond Flan (see page 69)

Little Christmas Tarts (see page 63)

Banana Cream Pie (see page 75)

Peach Cobbler (see page 74)

Baked Bread and Butter Pudding (see page 22)

Chocolate Pear Flan
Illustrated on page 65

**1 deep (20–25-cm/8–9-inch) shortcrust pastry
  case, baked (see page 58)**
1 level tablespoon powdered gelatine
1 level tablespoon cornflour
75 g/3 oz castor sugar
4 egg yolks
450 ml/¾ pint milk
75 g/3 oz bitter chocolate
vanilla essence
5-6 canned pear halves
apple jelly, sieved
**whipped cream and chopped bitter
  chocolate, to decorate**

1. Sprinkle powdered gelatine over 2 tablespoons
cold water in a cup and put aside to soften.

2. In the top of a double saucepan, stir cornflour
into castor sugar.

3. Beat egg yolks lightly, pour them over cornflour mixture, stirring vigorously with a wooden
spoon until smoothly blended.

4. Bring milk to the boil, pour in a thin stream
into egg mixture, stirring vigorously.

5. Cook over simmering water, for 15 to 20 minutes, stirring until custard coats back of spoon,
taking great care not to let it boil, or egg yolks
may curdle. Remove from heat.

6. Stand cup of softened gelatine in hot water (use
the water in the bottom of the double saucepan)
and stir until gelatine has dissolved and liquid is
clear. Blend thoroughly with custard.

7. Melt chocolate on a plate over simmering
water – yes, use the water left in the bottom of the
double saucepan.

8. Blend chocolate smoothly with hot custard and
flavour to taste with vanilla essence. Pour into
pastry case and chill until set on top.

9. Arrange 5 to 6 canned pear halves on chocolate
filling, cut sides uppermost. Brush pears with

sieved apple jelly to give them an attractive glaze,
and just before serving, pipe a little whipped
cream into each pear half and sprinkle with
chopped bitter chocolate.

Orange and Almond Flan
Illustrated on page 65

**1 23-cm/9-inch shortcrust pastry case, baked
  (see page 58)**

ALMOND FILLING
2 eggs
5 level tablespoons castor sugar
6 level tablespoons double cream
100 g/4 oz ground almonds
finely grated rind and juice of 1 large lemon
1-2 drops almond essence

ORANGE AND ALMOND TOPPING
4 small oranges
slivered almonds
apple jelly or greengage conserve, sieved

1. To prepare almond filling: whisk eggs with
sugar until thick and creamy. Add remaining
ingredients and beat vigorously with a wooden
spoon until smoothly blended.

2. Fill pastry case with almond mixture and bake
in a moderate oven (180°C, 350°F, Gas Mark 4)
for 15 to 20 minutes until puffed and golden, and
firm to the touch.

3. Peel 4 small oranges, removing all pith and
slice thinly. Arrange orange slices on top of the
flan in an overlapping circle. Fill centre with
slivered almonds. Brush orange slices with a little
sieved apple jelly or greengage conserve.

70

Sour Cream – Sultana Pie

225 g/8 oz sugar
½ level teaspoon powdered cinnamon
½ level teaspoon ground nutmeg or allspice
salt
2 eggs, beaten
300 ml/½ pint soured cream
2 tablespoons lemon juice
100 g/4 oz sultanas
1 (20–23-cm/8–9-inch) shortcrust pastry case,
  unbaked (see page 58)

1. Combine sugar, spices, salt, eggs, cream, lemon juice and sultanas. Mix until well blended.

2. Pour into pastry case and bake in a moderate oven (180°C, 350°F, Gas Mark 4) for 1 hour, or until filling has set. Cool.

American Custard Pie

1 level tablespoon cornflour
450 ml/¾ pint milk
grated rind of ½ lemon or orange
4–6 level tablespoons sugar
½ teaspoon vanilla essence
salt
3 eggs
1 (20–23-cm/8–9-inch) shortcrust pastry case,
  unbaked (see page 58)

1. Mix cornflour smoothly with a little milk. Combine remaining milk with lemon or orange rind in the top of a double saucepan and simmer gently over hot water for 15 minutes.

2. Strain hot milk into cornflour and return to double saucepan, cook over water, stirring constantly, until thickened. Add sugar, vanilla essence and salt, to taste. Cool.

3. Beat eggs and add to custard mixture. Mix well.

4. Prick base of unbaked pastry case with a fork. Cover with a piece of foil or waxed paper, weight this with dried beans and bake 'blind' in a hot oven (230°C, 450°F, Gas Mark 8) for 15 minutes. Remove foil and beans. Allow pastry case to cool.

5. Pour custard mixture into pastry case, sprinkle with ground nutmeg and bake in a moderately hot oven (190°C, 375°F, Gas Mark 5) for 25 to 30 minutes, until the pastry is cooked and the custard has set. Serve cooled but not chilled.

Variations

Cherry Custard Pie: Add to mixture 225 g/8 oz stoned unsweetened cherries soaked in 4 tablespoons cherry brandy (add the brandy, too) and bake as above.

Pear Custard Pie: Add to mixture 2 ripe pears (peeled, cored and thinly sliced) soaked in 4 to 6 tablespoons Kirsch (add Kirsch, too) and bake as above.

Apple Cream Pie

175 g/6 oz shortcrust pastry (see page 58),
  made with addition of 75 g/3 oz grated
  cheese
75 g/3 oz castor sugar
75 g/3 oz soft brown sugar
25 g/1 oz cornflour
½ level teaspoon ground cinnamon
¼ level teaspoon grated nutmeg
pinch of salt
40 g/1½ oz butter
8 tart cooking apples
2 teaspoons lemon juice
6 level tablespoons double cream

1. Make up shortcrust pastry, adding the cheese after the butter has been rubbed in. Roll out pastry and line a 20-cm/8-inch pie plate.

2. Mix together sugar, brown sugar, cornflour, cinnamon, nutmeg and salt in a bowl. Rub in the butter.

3. Peel, core and slice the apples and sprinkle with the lemon juice in a bowl. Add three-quarters of the sugar mixture and toss apples, coating them evenly.

4. Arrange coated apple slices in pastry case, piling them high in a dome, and sprinkle with remaining

sugar mixture. Bake in a hot oven (230°C, 450°F, Gas Mark 8) for 10 minutes, then reduce oven temperature to moderately hot (190°C, 375°F, Gas Mark 5) and continue baking for 25 minutes, until the apples are tender. Pour cream over the pie, and bake for 10 minutes longer. Serve immediately.

Chocolate Cream Pie

50 g/2 oz bitter chocolate
225 g/8 oz sugar
2 level tablespoons cornflour
¼ level teaspoon salt
450 ml/¾ pint milk
2 eggs, well beaten
2 level tablespoons butter
½ teaspoon vanilla essence
1 (23-cm/9-inch) shortcrust pastry case,
   baked (see page 58)

GARNISH
300 ml/½ pint double cream
50 g/2 oz sugar
½ teaspoon vanilla essence
15 g/½ oz bitter chocolate, coarsely grated

1. Melt chocolate over hot water in the top of a double saucepan.

2. Combine sugar, cornflour and salt in a bowl. Gradually stir in milk, then stir mixture into melted chocolate. Cook over boiling water for 10 minutes, stirring constantly until thick.

3. Pour hot mixture into well-beaten eggs a little at a time, stirring after each addition. Return to top of double saucepan and cook, stirring occasionally, for 5 minutes. Remove from heat, add butter and vanilla essence. Cool.

4. Pour mixture into baked pastry case.

5. To serve: whip cream and blend in the sugar and vanilla essence. Decorate pie with piped cream and sprinkle grated chocolate on top of the cream. Chill and serve.

Tartes aux Pêches

6 small peaches
225 g/8 oz sugar
150 ml/¼ pint water
ground cinnamon
150 ml/¼ pint red Burgundy
1 strip orange peel
2 tablespoons Grand Marnier or Curaçao
12 individual shortcrust pastry cases (see
   page 58)
whipped cream

1. Pour boiling water over peaches in a bowl, remove and peel. Slice in half and remove stones.

2. Poach peaches, uncovered, in syrup made of sugar, water, and cinnamon, to taste, for about 15 minutes. Add Burgundy and orange peel and continue to cook, uncovered, over a low heat until fruit is tender – about 15 minutes.

3. Put peaches in a deep bowl. Reduce liquid over high heat to the consistency of a thick syrup. Add Grand Marnier or Curaçao and pour syrup over the halved peaches. Put in the refrigerator to chill thoroughly.

4. Place a halved peach inside each pastry case. Glaze with the reduced syrup and garnish with rosettes of whipped cream.

72

Lemon Sponge Tart

3 level tablespoons butter
175 g/6 oz sugar
3 eggs, separated
3 level tablespoons plain flour
450 ml/¾ pint milk
juice of 3 lemons
grated rind of 1 lemon
1 (20–23-cm/8–9-inch) shortcrust pastry case,
   unbaked (see page 58)

1. Cream butter and blend with sugar and egg yolks until light and creamy.

2. Sprinkle with flour, then mix in milk, lemon juice and rind.

3. Whisk egg whites until stiff, fold into lemon mixture.

4. Pour lemon mixture into unbaked pastry case and bake in a moderate oven (180°C, 350°F, Gas Mark 4) for approximately 45 minutes.

Eggnog Pie

150 ml/¼ pint single cream
3 egg yolks
75 g/3 oz granulated sugar
salt and freshly grated nutmeg
1½ level teaspoons powdered gelatine
2 tablespoons cold water
2 tablespoons rum
1 tablespoon brandy
½ teaspoon vanilla essence
3 egg whites
150 ml/¼ pint double cream
1 (20–23-cm/8–9-inch) shortcrust pastry case,
   baked (see page 58)

1. Scald cream in the top of a double saucepan.

2. Combine egg yolks, sugar, salt and freshly grated nutmeg, and stir into the scalded cream. Cook over hot water until the mixture coats a spoon, stirring constantly.

3. Soften gelatine in water, add to custard mixture

and stir until dissolved. Add rum, brandy and vanilla essence and strain custard into a glass bowl. Chill until mixture begins to set.

4. Whisk egg whites until stiff and whip cream. Fold egg white and cream into custard mixture and pour into the baked pastry case. Chill.

5. Just before serving, sprinkle with a little freshly grated nutmeg.

Lemon Soufflé Pie

4 egg yolks, well beaten
175 g/6 oz sugar
4 tablespoons lemon juice
¼–½ level teaspoon ground nutmeg
1–2 level teaspoons grated lemon rind
1 teaspoon vanilla essence
salt
4 egg whites
1 (23-cm/9-inch) shortcrust pastry case,
   baked (see page 58)

1. Combine egg yolks, a third of the sugar, and lemon juice. Flavour to taste with nutmeg and cook over water, stirring constantly, until mixture thickens. Remove from heat. Mix in grated lemon rind and vanilla essence. Cool.

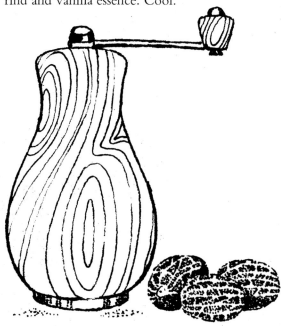

2. Add salt to egg whites and whisk until soft peaks form. Gradually add remaining sugar and whisk until stiff. Fold into warm lemon mixture.

3. Spoon mixture into baked pastry case and bake in a moderate oven (160°C, 325°F, Gas Mark 3) for about 30 minutes, or until golden brown.

Pears in Pastry Sabayon

6 pears
150 ml/¼ pint syrup (100 g/4 oz sugar,
   8 tablespoons water)
150 ml/¼ pint apricot jam
cream (optional)

PASTRY
250 g/9 oz plain flour
1 level teaspoon salt
4 level tablespoons lard
100 g/4 oz softened butter
water, to mix

SABAYON SAUCE
4 egg yolks
100 g/4 oz sugar
175 ml/6 fl oz Marsala
1-2 tablespoons cognac

1. To make pastry: sift flour and salt together, rub in lard and half the butter until mixture resembles fine breadcrumbs. Add sufficient water to form into a ball which will just hold together, and knead firmly but quickly until smooth. Allow to rest in a cool place for 15 minutes. Roll out into an oblong and spread remaining butter over surface. Fold in half, seal edges, rest for 5 minutes and roll out to 3-mm/⅛-inch thickness. Cut 6 pastry rounds large enough for pears to sit upon and cut remainder of pastry into strips about 1 cm/ ½ inch wide.

2. Peel pears and poach them whole in syrup and apricot jam for 10 to 15 minutes. Remove pears and cool. Reserve apricot syrup. Place one pear on each pastry round.

3. To make cage of pastry strips for each pear: cross two strips at right angles, seal well with

water and place cross at top of each pear. Snip strips at base and seal well with water.

4. Place pears in pastry on baking tray and bake in a moderately hot oven (200°C, 400°F, Gas Mark 6) for 20 to 30 minutes, until pastry is set. Remove and brush with apricot syrup glaze.

5. To make Sabayon sauce: beat egg yolks and sugar in the top of a double saucepan until yellow and frothy. Add Marsala, place over hot water and cook, stirring constantly, until thick and foamy. Stir in cognac and chill.

6. Serve pears with cream or Sabayon sauce.

Coffee Chiffon Flan

1 (23-cm/9-inch) rich shortcrust flan case,
   baked (see page 59)
1 level tablespoon powdered gelatine
4 tablespoons cold water
450 ml/¾ pint milk
4 eggs, separated
100 g/4 oz castor sugar
2 level tablespoons powdered coffee
150 ml/¼ pint double cream, whipped
¼ teaspoon salt
coarsely grated chocolate

1. Soak gelatine in cold water.

2. Warm the milk in a small saucepan.

3. Cream together egg yolks, half the sugar, and coffee. Pour on warm milk, stirring constantly. Return to heat and cook gently until custard just coats the spoon. Cool.

4. Dissolve softened gelatine over gentle heat and stir into cooled coffee custard. Fold in whipped cream.

5. Whisk egg whites with salt until stiff but not dry, then whisk in remaining sugar a little at a time.

6. Whisk coffee custard and fold gradually into beaten egg whites. Turn into baked flan case and decorate with coarsely grated chocolate.

74

Peach Cobbler
Illustrated on page 68

PASTRY
225 g/8 oz plain flour, sifted
25 g/1 oz cornflour
1 level teaspoon salt
175 g/6 oz butter
4 tablespoons water

FILLING
225 g/8 oz sugar
2 level tablespoons cornflour
2 tablespoons butter
450 ml/$\frac{3}{4}$ pint peach juice
6 peaches, sliced
1 tablespoon lemon juice

1. To make pastry: combine sifted flour, cornflour, salt, butter and water in a bowl. Mix well into a dough. Line a large deep dish with the pastry, reserving enough for lattice topping.

2. To make filling: combine sugar, cornflour and butter with peach juice. Cook until thick – about 5 minutes. Add lemon juice and pour over peaches.

3. Pour filling into pastry case. Dot with butter. Top with strips of pastry and bake in a moderate oven (160°C, 325°F, Gas Mark 3) for 30 minutes.

Peach Pie with Streusel Topping

6 peaches
juice of 1 lemon
**1 (20-23-cm/8-9-inch) shortcrust pastry case,
   unbaked (see page 58)**
50 g/2 oz sugar
$\frac{1}{2}$ level teaspoon powdered cinnamon
$\frac{1}{4}$ level teaspoon ground nutmeg or allspice

STREUSEL TOPPING
75 g/3 oz brown sugar
75 g/3 oz plain flour, sifted
grated rind of 1 lemon
6 tablespoons softened butter

1. Peel and slice peaches discarding stones and toss in lemon juice.

2. Arrange prepared peaches in unbaked pastry case. Combine sugar and spices, and sprinkle over peaches.

3. To make streusel topping: combine brown sugar, flour and grated lemon rind, and cut softened butter into mixture until crumbly, with a pastry blender or 2 knives.

4. Sprinkle mixture over peaches and bake in a hot oven (230°C, 450°F, Gas Mark 8) for 15 minutes. Reduce oven temperature to moderate (180°C, 350°F, Gas Mark 4) and bake for a further 30 minutes.

Autumn Pear Flan

I (23-cm/9-inch) rich shortcrust flan case,
   baked (see page 59)
6-8 pears

PASTRY CREAM
100 g/4 oz sugar
4 level tablespoons cornflour
450 ml/$\frac{3}{4}$ pint milk
5 egg yolks
$\frac{1}{2}$-1 teaspoon vanilla essence
2 teaspoons Kirsch

WINE SYRUP
175 g/6 oz sugar
300 ml/$\frac{1}{2}$ pint red wine
grated rind of 1 lemon
4 cloves
2.5-cm/1-inch piece of root ginger
1-1$\frac{1}{2}$ teaspoons red food colouring
1 level teaspoon gelatine
4 tablespoons cold water
juice of 1 lemon
150 ml/$\frac{1}{4}$ pint thick unsweetened apple purée

1. To make pastry cream: combine sugar and
cornflour in the top of a double saucepan. Stir in
milk and cook over direct heat, stirring all the
time, until mixture comes to the boil. Boil for 1
minute. Beat yolks slightly, add a little hot milk
mixture and pour back into milk and sugar mixture. Cook over hot but not boiling water, until
thickened – 5 to 10 minutes, stirring continuously.
Strain and cool. Add vanilla essence and Kirsch.
Cover with waxed paper and refrigerate until
well chilled.

2. Peel and core pears.

3. Dissolve sugar in wine with lemon rind, cloves
and ginger. Bring to the boil and cook for 3
minutes. Reduce heat to simmering point, stir in
red food colouring and poach pears very gently,
turning occasionally, until tender but not mushy.
Remove from syrup and cool.

4. Soak gelatine in cold water and add with
lemon juice and apple purée to the hot syrup. Mix
thoroughly until smooth, cool.

5. Half fill flan case with pastry cream. Arrange
pears on top and cover with red apple-wine sauce.

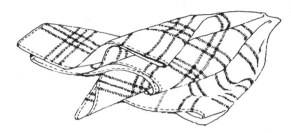

Banana Cream Pie
Illustrated on page 68

I (20-23-cm/8-9-inch) shortcrust or rich
   biscuit crust pastry case, baked (see
   pages 58, 59)
3 bananas, sliced
juice of 1 lemon
150 ml/$\frac{1}{4}$ pint double cream, whipped

VANILLA ICE CREAM
100 g/4 oz sugar
3 level tablespoons cornflour
450 ml/$\frac{3}{4}$ pint milk
5 egg yolks
$\frac{1}{2}$-1 teaspoon vanilla essence
2 teaspoons Kirsch

1. To make vanilla ice cream: combine sugar
and cornflour in the top of a double saucepan. Stir
in milk and cook over direct heat, stirring constantly, until mixture comes to the boil. Boil for 1
minute. Beat egg yolks slightly and pan in a little
hot milk mixture. Return to the milk and sugar
mixture and cook over hot but not boiling water
until thickened – 5 to 10 minutes, stirring continuously. Strain and cool, then add vanilla
essence and Kirsch.

2. Combine sliced bananas and lemon juice in a
shallow bowl and toss.

3. Place a third of drained banana slices in a layer
in the bottom of baked pastry case. Cover with
half the vanilla ice cream and arrange another
third of banana slices on top. Cover with remaining vanilla ice cream. Top pie decoratively with
remaining banana slices and decorate with
whipped cream. Serve cold but not chilled.

Cakes

Basic Sponge Cake

slightly softened butter
100 g/4 oz castor sugar
¼ teaspoon vanilla essence
¼ level teaspoon finely grated lemon rind
2 eggs
100 g/4 oz plain flour
1 level teaspoon baking powder
redcurrant jam or a flavoured butter icing
icing sugar

1. Lightly butter two 18-cm/7-inch sandwich tins and line bases with circles of *very* lightly buttered greaseproof paper.

2. Combine butter with the castor sugar, vanilla essence and finely grated lemon rind in a large bowl. Cream together with a wooden spoon until light and fluffy.

3. In another bowl whisk eggs until light and frothy. Beat whisked eggs, a few tablespoons at a time into creamed butter and sugar mixture.

4. Sift flour and baking powder into creamed mixture. Fold in lightly but thoroughly with a metal spoon or spatula.

5. Divide batter evenly between prepared sandwich tins and level off tops with your spatula.

6. Bake in a moderate oven (180°C, 350°F, Gas Mark 4) for 25 minutes or until a good golden brown. The cakes are cooked when they shrink away slightly from the sides of the tin and spring back when pressed lightly with a finger.

Note: Always place baking tins in the centre of the oven. And if you are using 2 rungs, it is a good idea to switch the two tins over two-thirds of the way through cooking time to allow them to brown evenly.

7. When cakes are done, turn out on to a folded cloth and carefully peel off base papers. Then turn right side up again and allow to cool on a wire tray.

8. When layers are cold, sandwich with warm redcurrant jam or a rich chocolate- or butterscotch-flavoured butter icing and top with a sprinkling of icing sugar.

are lifted (3 to 5 minutes if beating with an electric mixer at high speed).

7. Gradually resift flour and cornflour mixture over surface, at the same time folding it in lightly but thoroughly with a large metal spoon or spatula.

8. Add 8 tablespoons melted butter and continue with the folding motion until it has been completely absorbed. This may take slightly longer than you expect, so work as lightly as you can to avoid knocking the air out of the mixture.

9. Divide batter evenly between prepared tins.

10. Bake in a moderate oven (180°C, 350°F, Gas Mark 4) for 15 to 20 minutes, until cakes are well risen, golden brown on top and springy to the touch.

11. Turn out on to wire trays. Peel off lining paper and allow cakes to cool completely before using.

American Refrigerator Cake

2 (18-cm/7-inch) sponge cakes (see preceding recipes)
600 ml/1 pint double cream
4-6 level tablespoons cocoa
4 tablespoons hot water
2-4 tablespoons crème de cacao
icing sugar

1. Split each sponge layer in half to make two layers each.

2. Whip double cream until thickened. Dissolve cocoa in hot water and cool. Then beat into whipped cream. Add *crème de cacao* and icing sugar, to taste.

3. Spread cocoa cream between layers and on top and sides of cake. Chill cake for at least 1 hour in the refrigerator.

Basic Genoese Sponge Cake

(Excellent for layer cakes, iced cakes and *petits fours*.)

75 g/3 oz plain flour
25 g/1 oz cornflour
about 150 g/5 oz unsalted butter
4 eggs
100 g/4 oz castor sugar
1 teaspoon vanilla essence or finely grated rind of $\frac{1}{2}$ lemon

1. Sift flour with cornflour three times.

2. Take the mixing bowl in which you intend to whisk up the cake and select a large saucepan over which it will fit firmly. Pour 5 cm/2 inches water into the saucepan and bring to the boil.

3. Place unsalted butter in another, smaller saucepan and lower into the heating water, so that the butter melts without sizzling or bubbling. Remove saucepan from water.

4. Brush two 19- or 20-cm/7$\frac{1}{2}$- or 8-inch sandwich tins with a little of the melted butter. Line bases with greaseproof paper and brush with melted butter as well.

5. Combine eggs, castor sugar and vanilla essence or grated lemon rind in a mixing bowl. Set it over the barely simmering water and whisk vigorously until very thick, light and lukewarm.

6. Remove bowl from heat. Stand bowl on a cool surface and continue to whisk until mixture leaves a distinct trail on the surface when beaters

78 | **Baked Almond Apples**

4 large apples
lemon juice
cornflour
50 g/2 oz blanched almonds
100 g/4 oz sugar
50 g/2 oz butter
1 egg
40 g/1½ oz cakecrumbs

1. Peel and core apples, brush with lemon juice and roll in cornflour.

2. Chop almonds and mix with half the sugar.

3. Melt butter in an ovenproof dish, put in apples and fill centres with almond and sugar mixture.

4. Beat egg and rest of sugar together and stir in 25 g/1 oz cakecrumbs.

5. Mix any left-over almond and sugar mixture (Step 3) with egg, sugar and cakecrumbs and pour over the apples.

6. Sprinkle remaining 15 g/½ oz breadcrumbs on top and bake in a moderately hot oven (190°C, 375°F, Gas Mark 5) until tender, approximately 45 minutes.

Pear Clafouti

50 g/2 oz flour
pinch of salt
2 eggs, beaten
300 ml/½ pint milk
4 ripe pears
50 g/2 oz castor sugar
juice of ½ lemon
1 level teaspoon powdered cinnamon
melted butter
icing sugar

1. Sift flour and salt into a mixing bowl, make a well in the centre and pour in the eggs. Stir thoroughly, gradually adding the milk, and beat well.

2. Peel, core and slice the pears and mix with sugar, lemon juice and cinnamon.

3. Grease a 20-cm/8-inch baking dish or cake tin. Stir three-quarters of the pears into the batter and pour into the tin, arrange remaining pears over top, and brush these with melted butter. Bake in a moderate oven (180°C, 350°F, Gas Mark 4) for 40 minutes. Serve dredged with icing sugar.

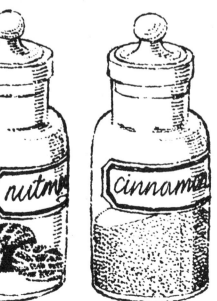

Christmas Spice Cookies

Illustrated on page 88

225 g/8 oz flour, sifted
½ level teaspoon salt
½ level teaspoon bicarbonate of soda
½ level teaspoon baking powder
½ level teaspoon ground ginger
½ level teaspoon cloves
1½ level teaspoons powdered cinnamon
¼ level teaspoon freshly ground nutmeg
4-6 level tablespoons softened butter
100 g/4 oz granulated sugar
250 ml/8 fl oz golden syrup
1 egg yolk

SUGAR ICING
175 g/6 oz icing sugar
⅛ level teaspoon cream of tartar
1 egg white
¼ teaspoon vanilla essence
food colouring

DECORATION
coloured sugar
candies
silver balls
chocolate chips
nuts
raisins

1. Sift flour with salt, bicarbonate of soda, baking powder and spices into a bowl.

2. Beat butter, sugar and syrup until creamy. Add egg yolk and beat well. Blend in flour mixture.

3. Roll out dough 3-5 mm/⅛-¼ inch thick on a lightly floured board. With floured biscuit cutters, cut into different shapes. Place cookies on an ungreased baking sheet, 2.5 cm/1 inch apart. Bake in a moderate oven (180°C, 350°F, Gas Mark 4) for 8 to 10 minutes, until cooked. Beat sugar icing ingredients together, and when cookies are cold decorate with piped icing. Trim with coloured sugar, candies, silver balls, chocolate chips, nuts, raisins, etc.

4. To make sugar icing for cookies: sift icing sugar with cream of tartar. Add egg white and vanilla essence. Then with a rotary beater or electric mixer, beat mixture until icing holds its shape.

Note: To prevent icing from setting while you are decorating cookies, cover bowl with a damp cloth. Colour icing, as desired.

80

Sicilian Cassata Cake

100 g/4 oz glacé fruit, chopped
4 tablespoons Strega liqueur or brandy
350 g/12 oz Ricotta cream cheese or cottage cheese
100 g/4 oz vanilla-flavoured sugar
100 g/4 oz plain eating chocolate (slightly bitter if possible), chopped
butter
sponge fingers, halved

ICING
350 g/12 oz bitter chocolate
2 level tablespoons softened butter
3 tablespoons milk

DECORATION
candied cherries
whipped cream
angelica leaves (optional)

1. Place chopped glacé fruit in a small bowl; add *Strega* liqueur or brandy, and allow fruits to marinate in the liqueur for at least 1 hour.

2. Sieve the cheese into a large earthenware mixing bowl. Add the vanilla-flavoured sugar, working the mixture with a wooden spoon until you have a smooth, fluffy cream. Drain the chopped fruits, reserving liqueur, then stir the fruits and chocolate into cream.

3. Line a long narrow loaf (or pâté) tin with waxed paper. Spread lightly with softened butter. Line the tin, sides and bottom, with halved sponge fingers cut to fit (round sides of fingers facing outside of tin), saving enough halved sponge fingers to cover the top of the cake. Spoon in the mixture until just under half-full. Add trimmings and ends of sponge fingers, diced and soaked in remaining liqueur (adding a little extra liqueur if necessary). Then top with remaining cream mixture. Cover with reserved halved sponge fingers and chill in refrigerator for at least 2 hours.

4. When ready to serve, turn the sweet out and carefully remove waxed paper.

5. **To make icing:** melt the chocolate and butter in a small saucepan over water, stirring until smooth. Add enough milk to make it of coating consistency, then coat each sponge finger.

6. **To decorate:** place half a candied cherry between each sponge finger all around the top of the rectangular cake, then decorate with whipped cream and 'leaves' of angelica.

Poire Vefour

4-6 ripe fresh pears

VANILLA SYRUP
450 ml/$\frac{3}{4}$ pint water
225 g/8 oz sugar
few drops of vanilla essence

PASTRY CREAM
175 g/6 oz sugar
3 level tablespoons flour
2$\frac{1}{2}$ level tablespoons cornflour
450 ml/$\frac{3}{4}$ pint milk
6 egg yolks
6 level tablespoons butter
vanilla essence
Grand Marnier

GARNISH
macaroon halves
Grand Marnier
150 ml/$\frac{1}{4}$ pint double cream, whipped
sugar
crystallised violets

1. **To prepare pears:** peel, core and cut in half. Poach in vanilla syrup. Allow to cool.

2. **To make vanilla syrup:** dissolve water, sugar and vanilla essence over a low heat. Simmer until of a syrupy consistency.

3. **To make pastry cream:** combine sugar, flour and cornflour in the top of a double saucepan. Stir in milk and cook over direct heat, stirring all the time, until mixture comes to the boil. Boil for 1 minute. Beat egg yolks lightly and add a little hot milk mixture. Return to the saucepan with milk and sugar mixture, stirring constantly. Cook over

Walnut Butter Cookies

225 g/8 oz plain flour, sifted
100 g/4 oz granulated sugar
$\frac{1}{4}$–$\frac{1}{2}$ level teaspoon salt
$\frac{1}{4}$ level teaspoon powdered cinnamon
2 level teaspoons instant coffee
225 g/8 oz butter, diced
225 g/8 oz walnuts, chopped

1. Place flour, granulated sugar, salt, cinnamon and instant coffee into a medium-sized mixing bowl.

2. Add diced butter to a bowl and cut in with a pastry blender or knife until butter is the size of very small peas.

3. Press dough together and knead once or twice. Divide dough into small balls and then roll each ball in chopped walnuts.

4. Place balls on an ungreased baking tray about 2.5 cm/1 inch apart. Flatten each ball using the bottom of a tablespoon dipped in granulated sugar. Put a few more chopped nuts on to each side. Bake in a moderate oven (160°C, 325°F, Gas Mark 3) for 20 minutes, or until the edges are crisp and lightly browned. Cool and remove to wire tray.

hot but not boiling water, for 5 minutes, stirring constantly. Strain and allow to cool slightly. Stir in the butter and flavour to taste with vanilla essence and Grand Marnier.

4. To assemble dish: spread the bottom of a serving dish with half of the pastry cream. Allow to cool. Garnish with macaroon halves which you have sprinkled lightly with Grand Marnier. Cover lightly with remaining pastry cream and arrange poached pear halves on top.

5. Sweeten whipped cream with a little sugar and Grand Marnier, to taste. Decorate dish with cream and crystallised violets.

Cherry Cheesecake

Illustrated on page 85

Canned cherries may be used to make this cheese-cake when fresh ones are out of season, but if you do use them, you may have to use less sugar (or more lemon) in the cheese filling, and sharpen the flavour of the glaze with a little lemon juice as well.

BISCUIT BASE
175 g/6 oz digestive biscuits
50 g/2 oz softened butter

FILLING
350 g/12 oz ripe fresh cherries, halved and stoned
175 g/6 oz cream cheese
225 g/8 oz cottage cheese
4 level tablespoons castor sugar
1 teaspoon vanilla essence
finely grated rind and juice of 1 lemon
2 egg yolks, beaten
1 level tablespoon powdered gelatine
300 ml/½ pint double cream
2 egg whites

TOPPING
50 g/2 oz sugar
450 g/1 lb fresh cherries, halved and stoned
2 level tablespoons cherry jam, sieved
1 level tablespoon toasted flaked almonds

1. To make biscuit crust: crush biscuits finely and blend with softened butter. Press mixture evenly into a 20-cm/8-inch, loose-bottomed cake tin. Bake in a moderate oven (160°C, 325°F, Gas Mark 3) for 10 minutes. Remove from oven and allow to cool.

2. To make filling: put halved, stoned cherries in a saucepan with 150 ml/¼ pint water. Bring to the boil and simmer, mashing occasionally with a wooden spoon, until cherries are reduced to a pulp. Cool and drain off excess liquid.

3. Combine cheeses, sugar and vanilla essence in a large bowl. Add lemon juice, grated lemon rind and beaten egg yolks, and whisk until smooth.

4. Soften gelatine in 2 tablespoons cold water in a small cup. Place cup in a bowl of hot water and stir until gelatine has completely dissolved. Add to cheese mixture and blend thoroughly.

5. Whip cream lightly and fold into mixture, together with cherry pulp.

6. Whisk egg whites until stiff but not dry and fold gently into cheese mixture.

7. Spoon cheese mixture over biscuit base, and chill in the refrigerator until set.

8. To make topping: dissolve sugar in 300 ml/½ pint water over a low heat. Poach cherries in this syrup until just cooked, 10 to 15 minutes, depending on ripeness. Drain fruit, reserving syrup. Remove skins carefully, pat cherry halves dry and arrange them on top of chilled cheesecake, close together.

9. Add sieved cherry jam to syrup and spoon over top of cheesecake. Sprinkle with toasted flaked almonds. Serve very cold.

German Cheesecake

PASTRY BASE
175 g/6 oz plain flour
100 g/4 oz softened butter
50 g/2 oz castor sugar
1 egg yolk
¼ level teaspoon finely grated lemon rind

CHEESE FILLING
50 g/2 oz sultanas
1-2 tablespoons dark rum
225 g/8 oz cottage cheese
150 ml/¼ pint soured cream
4 eggs, separated
1 level teaspoon finely grated lemon rind
100 g/4 oz castor sugar
1 level tablespoon plain flour, sifted

1. To make pastry case: sift flour into a large bowl and make a well in the centre.

2. In another bowl, cream butter and sugar together, until light and fluffy.

3. Blend in the egg yolk and finely grated lemon rind.

4. Finally, work in flour to make a smooth, soft dough.

5. Press dough evenly over the base of a deep, loose-bottomed 18-cm/7-inch cake tin.

6. Bake in a moderate oven (160°C, 325°F, Gas Mark 3) for 20 minutes or until firm but not coloured.

7. Remove pastry base from oven and allow to cool in the tin. At the same time, reduce oven temperature to cool (140°C, 275°F, Gas Mark 1).

8. To make cheese filling: toss sultanas in rum in a small bowl and leave to infuse until required.

9. Rub cottage cheese through a fine sieve into a large bowl.

10. Beat in soured cream, egg yolks and finely grated lemon rind until smoothly blended.

11. Whisk egg whites until stiff but not dry. Then gradually whisk in castor sugar and sifted flour, and continue to whisk until meringue is stiff and glossy.

12. With a large metal spoon or spatula, carefully fold meringue into cheese mixture.

13. Spoon mixture over baked pastry case. Sprinkle surface with rum-soaked sultanas.

14. Bake cheesecake in the cool oven for 40 to 50 minutes until firm to the touch.

15. Cool, remove from tin and chill lightly before serving.

84

Summer Orange Cake

Illustrated on page 87

CAKE
6 eggs, separated
175 g/6 oz sugar
2 tablespoons water
grated rind of 1 orange
generous pinch of salt
75 g/3 oz flour
25 g/1 oz cornflour

ORANGE TOPPING
1 egg
150 g/5 oz sugar
grated rind and juice of 1 orange made up
  to 150 ml/¼ pint with water
25 g/1 oz flour
300 ml/½ pint double cream, whipped
100 g/4 oz chopped toasted almonds
candied orange slices

1. To make cake: beat egg yolks, sugar, water, orange rind and salt until light and fluffy (5 minutes in mixer at high speed). Sift flour and cornflour, and gradually blend into egg yolk mixture. Whisk egg whites until stiff but not dry and fold gently into yolk mixture. Place equal quantities of mixture into three round 20-cm/8-inch cake tins which have been buttered and lightly dusted with flour. Bake in a moderate oven (180°C, 350°F, Gas Mark 4) for 45 minutes, or until golden brown. Invert layers on wire racks. When cool, loosen edges and remove from pans.

2. To make topping: beat egg, sugar and orange rind together until foamy; add sifted flour and orange juice, and cook in the top of a double saucepan, stirring all the time, until smooth and thick. Cool. Fold in whipped cream. Spread 2 cake layers with orange topping and put together. Cover top and sides of cake with topping and pat chopped almonds firmly around the sides. Decorate with candied orange slices.

Note: Alternatively the cake may be baked in a single cake tin and the almonds omitted in the decoration.

Chocolate Pear Meringues

3 large pears
150 ml/¼ pint lemon juice
40 g/1½ oz granulated sugar
2 level tablespoons redcurrant jelly
2 egg whites
100 g/4 oz castor sugar

SAUCE
75 g/3 oz unsweetened chocolate
50 g/2 oz sugar
1–2 level teaspoons cocoa
300 ml/½ pint water
vanilla essence
2 egg yolks

1. Peel and core the pears, cut them in half and simmer gently in water with a squeeze of lemon juice. Do not allow them to break. Drain and place in a buttered ovenproof dish.

2. Put the rest of the lemon juice, granulated sugar and redcurrant jelly into saucepan and bring to the boil. Pour over the pears.

3. Whisk egg whites stiffly and fold in the castor sugar. Pipe in circles around the top of each pear, leaving cavity of each pear visible. Bake meringued pears in a cool oven (150°C, 300°F, Gas Mark 2) for 15 to 20 minutes, until lightly browned.

4. To make chocolate sauce: break up chocolate and reserve 1 small piece. Put the rest into a small pan with sugar, cocoa and water. Stir until boiling, and the chocolate has dissolved. Simmer for about 15 minutes, until syrupy. Add vanilla essence and stir in egg yolks, off the heat. Fill centres of pears with this sauce, and grate the reserved chocolate on top. Serve remaining sauce separately.

Cherry Cheesecake (see page 82)

Summer Orange Cake (see page 84)

Christmas Spice Cookies (see page 79)

Summer Almond Cake

CAKE
6 eggs, separated
175 g/6 oz sugar
2 tablespoons water
grated rind of 1 lemon
generous pinch of salt
75 g/3 oz flour
25 g/1 oz cornflour

LEMON TOPPING
1 egg
150 g/5 oz sugar
grated rind and juice of 1 lemon made up to 150 ml/$\frac{1}{4}$ pint with water
25 g/1 oz flour
300 ml/$\frac{1}{2}$ pint double cream, whipped
100 g/4 oz chopped toasted almonds

1. To make cake: beat egg yolks, sugar, water, lemon rind and salt until light and fluffy (5 minutes in mixer at high speed). Sift flour and cornflour, and gradually blend into egg yolk mixture. Whisk egg whites until stiff but not dry and fold gently into yolk mixture. Place equal quantities of mixture into three 20-cm/8-inch round cake tins which have been buttered and lightly dusted with flour. Bake in a moderate oven (180°C, 350°F, Gas Mark 4) for 45 minutes, or until golden brown. Invert layers on wire racks. When cool, loosen edges and remove from pans.

2. To make topping: beat egg, sugar and lemon rind together until foamy; add sifted flour and lemon juice, and cook in the top of a double saucepan, stirring all the time, until smooth and thick. Cool. Fold in whipped cream. Spread 2 cake layers with lemon topping and put together. Cover top and sides of cake with topping and pat chopped almonds firmly around sides.

American Devil's Foodcake

89

3 tablespoons cocoa
3 level tablespoons sugar
3 tablespoons water
150 ml/$\frac{1}{4}$ pint milk
1 teaspoon vanilla essence
100 g/4 oz butter
225 g/8 oz brown sugar
3 egg yolks
75 g/3 oz plain flour
25 g/1 oz cornflour
1 level teaspoon bicarbonate of soda
pinch of salt
3 egg whites, stiffly beaten

CHOCOLATE FILLING AND ICING
175 g/6 oz plain chocolate
8 tablespoons double cream
50 g/2 oz butter
450 g/1 lb icing sugar, sifted

1. Combine cocoa, sugar and water in the top of a double saucepan, and cook over water, stirring, until smooth and thick. Stir in milk and vanilla essence, blend well and set aside to cool.

2. Cream butter and sugar. Beat in egg yolks one at a time, then beat in chocolate mixture.

3. Sift flour and cornflour three times with bicarbonate of soda and salt, and beat into cake mixture. Fold in egg whites. Butter and lightly dust with flour three 20-cm/8-inch sandwich tins. Pour cake mixture into prepared tins and bake in a moderate oven (180°C, 350°F, Gas Mark 4) for 30 to 35 minutes.

4. To make chocolate filling and icing: melt chocolate with cream and butter in a double saucepan over hot water. When smooth, add sifted icing sugar. Mix well. Cool slightly and spread between cake layers and over top and sides of cake.

Sauces

Brandy Sauce *Makes 300 ml/½ pint*
Brandy Butter *Makes 225 g/8 oz*
Hot Chocolate Sauce *Makes 450 ml/¾ pint*

90

Brandy Sauce

4 egg yolks
4 level tablespoons double cream
4 tablespoons brandy
2 level tablespoons castor sugar

1. Combine all the ingredients in the top of a double saucepan. Add 4 tablespoons water.

2. Place pan over lightly simmering water and whisk for 6 to 8 minutes to make a thick, frothy sauce. Do not allow sauce to boil or it will curdle.

3. Serve warm or cold.

Brandy Butter

100 g/4 oz butter
100 g/4 oz castor sugar
2 tablespoons brandy

1. Soften butter with a wooden spoon, then beat until smooth and fluffy.

2. Put aside 1 level tablespoon castor sugar and gradually add remainder to creamed butter, beating vigorously until mixture is very fluffy and almost white.

3. Soak remaining sugar in brandy. Incorporate into butter cream a little at a time, and beat until smooth again. Chill until firm.

Hot Chocolate Sauce

50 g/2 oz bitter chocolate
300 ml/½ pint water
225 g/8 oz sugar
1 tablespoon cornflour
salt
2 tablespoons butter
2 tablespoons cognac
½ teaspoon very finely grated orange rind

1. Combine chocolate with water and melt over a gentle heat. When smooth add sugar, cornflour and salt. Cook, stirring continually, until sugar is dissolved and sauce is thick. Allow to boil for 3 minutes, then add butter and cognac and stir until smooth.

2. Remove from heat and add finely grated orange rind.

Apricot Sauce *Makes 300 ml/½ pint*
Vanilla Custard Sauce *Makes 450 ml/¾ pint*
Lemon or Strawberry Hard Sauce *Makes 450 g/1 lb*

Apricot Sauce

6-8 canned apricot halves
sugar
1 teaspoon cornflour
150 ml/¼ pint water
1-2 tablespoons Grand Marnier
2-3 drops of red food colouring

1. Make apricot purée by sieving canned apricots through a fine sieve or by liquidising in an electric blender, and add sugar to taste.

2. Combine purée with cornflour which you have dissolved in cold water, and heat in the top of a double saucepan until it boils and thickens. Add Grand Marnier and a few drops of red food colouring, and simmer for 2 to 3 minutes longer.

Vanilla Custard Sauce

91

450 ml/¾ pint milk
½ teaspoon vanilla essence
4 tablespoons sugar
4 egg yolks
¼ teaspoon salt

1. Simmer milk for 5 minutes then stir in vanilla essence.

2. Combine sugar, egg yolks and salt in a mixing bowl, and beat until fluffy and lemon-coloured.

3. Pour a little of the hot milk into the egg and sugar mixture, blend well, and then stir into the hot milk. Heat slowly in the top of a double saucepan, stirring constantly, until the mixture coats the back of a spoon. Serve warm.

To make Ginger Sauce: add 4 level tablespoons of finely chopped preserved ginger, and ginger syrup, to taste.

Lemon or Strawberry Hard Sauce

100 g/4 oz butter
350 g/12 oz icing sugar
grated rind and juice of 1 lemon or
    100 g/4 oz mashed strawberries

1. Work butter until soft, stir in icing sugar gradually and beat until smooth.

2. Stir in grated rind and juice of lemon, or mashed strawberries, and mix until smooth. Add more sugar if desired. Should sauce separate after standing, beat until well blended.

Index